FARMERS
MARKET
COOK
BOOK

Susan F. Carlman

CHICAGO REVIEW PRESS

Library of Congress Cataloging-in-Publication Data

Carlman, Susan F.
  Farmers market cookbook.

  Includes index.
  1. Cookery (Vegetables) 2. Cookery (Fruit)
I. Title.
TX801.C335   1988   641.6′5   88-2613
ISBN 1-55652-029-8 (pbk.)

*For Ruthann, who showed me that there is joy
in all things— surely not the least of them food*

Published by Chicago Review Press, Incorporated,
  814 N. Franklin, Chicago, IL 60610
ISBN: 1-55652-029-8

CONTENTS

ACKNOWLEDGMENTS

I have been lucky enough in my lifetime to cross paths with many wonderful folks, without some of whom this book might not have seen print.

Most important, and central to my being at this stage of my life, are my husband Dan and our two little omnivores, Erin and Sam. Their love, patience, and willingness to wait for supper helped provide the impetus to keep my pen scribbling.

Beyond our little family of four stretches a vast network of relations, scattered from Boston to Jackson Hole, from Fort Lauderdale to Detroit. The wonderful diversity of this very extended family is underscored by a common appreciation of good food which has laid an excellent foundation for building a career of exploring all things edible.

My dear pal Elizabeth offered support, gentle suggestions, and lots of inspiration to help me through the many major and minor details of this project. I can only hope one day to become half the cook Beth is.

The people at The Doings Newspapers in Hinsdale, Illinois, were the first ones to suggest that my dabbling with the spoon might be transcribed into readable copy. Without their encouragement and resources, this book still would be well beyond my grasp.

Finally, none of these ramblings would have been possible without the people who bring the bounty to market: the farmers. People like Tony Nichols (our cover model), Doris and Adolph Dongvillo, Darrel Bowen, and Waneta Biernacki offered invaluable guidance and answered a thousand questions with their genuine warmth and expertise. To all of these gracious individuals I will always owe my deepest appreciation.

INTRODUCTION

To Market, To Market,
To Buy a Fat Tomato

It's not just another item on your list of the day's errands. You can't lump it in with picking up the drapes at the cleaners and mailing off Cousin Sylvia's birthday present.

It's more than that. Part ritual, part necessity, the farmers market is a timeless event, a joyous celebration of the bounty of the earth beneath us. With exacting loyalty, the soil perenially pours forth a cornucopia of toothsome goods, brought to market with equal devotion by the people who plant and harvest them.

Where else can you go to buy a basket of plump, succulent raspberries from the guy who grew them, the two of you standing in the same brilliant sunlight that nurtured them to scarlet perfection?

Shopping for produce at a farmers market somehow brings one into closer touch with the cosmic chain which links us with the sun and the rain, the soil and the plant realm, the ashes and dust. We have bought the earth's yield at outdoor markets since the barter system first appeared in the shadow of the last glacial retreat. And of course, the open-air market still is the norm in many parts of the world.

When you take your fruits and vegetables from the farmer's table, chances are you are buying produce at its peak of freshness. Often the farmer will swear that it was picked while the flatbed truck was warming up at dawn today. Curb your skepticism a bit; he's probably telling the truth, or almost.

In buying from the grower you bypass the buyers, suppliers, distribution centers, and other pit stops made by most supermarket produce—at the expense of days' worth of precious ripeness. And although the prices may be equal to or a little higher than the supermarkets', during this period of trouble for the American farm, there is some satisfaction to be had in putting your money right into the grower's hands. Besides, the grower often is the best source of advice about cooking methods. Who better to ask how to cook a Hubbard squash than someone who brings truckloads of them to you every summer?

In preparation, one finds that perfectly fresh fruits and vegetables generally have little tolerance for pretense. Mostly they yearn to be loved for themselves: minimally adorned and cooked in a flash, if at all.

But now and then one runs across a tidbit of accompaniment or a special handling technique which helps the crop to take on untold new potential. And with fresh produce, the flavor possibilities can vary according to the ripeness of the item. Like people, vegetables carry certain virtues commensurate with each stage of life.

In this book, we will take a trip through the market season. Use these pages as a guide for the annual cook's tour which extends from asparagus to zucchini, and way beyond. Starting with the first tender morsels of spring greenery and sampling our way through the last crisp, golden days of autumn, we'll explore the many facets of the local harvest.

In general, we'll be dealing with crops in ways to which they are best suited, an approach which the Japanese describe with the concept of *shun*. This perspective allows the individual to make the most of the food as it is today, whether perfection is at hand or in the past.

Recipes are arranged according to the starring vegetable or fruit. Where there are several recipes given for the crop, the first one or two usually will be best for farm-fresh goods, the last ones more suited to foods you should have used up yesterday. (At the market, it's not uncommon to become so carried away that you buy more than you—and a dozen of your relatives—realistically can be expected to eat.)

Most dishes do have a starring crop, but because many of them include assorted supporting players, you'll need to check the index for any wayward listings. Often it's not one food which makes the dish, but rather several crops sharing the bill.

And because you'll be working with some of the finest raw materials available to you, it stands to reason that the rest of your ingredients should be top quality as well. If you want your food to be the absolute best it can be, try to see that your soup stocks are homemade and your pepper, spices, and cheeses freshly grated or ground. And other perishable goods, of course, cannot be expected to offer their utmost unless they are used when truly fresh.

So here we go. Market baskets firmly hooked in our elbows, minds resolutely opened, we are headed out for a marketing odyssey. We will do our best to take full advantage of the yield—to wade efficiently and deliciously through the tidal wave of fresh goods which floods our kitchens every summer.

But regrettably, we will not be able to do it all. Because the farmer today brings such a hugh variety of produce to market, we inevitably will overlook some items. The crops found in this book mostly will be those you can find not only in Detroit's Eastern Market and the Daley Plaza market in the heart of Chicago, but also under the umbrellas at markets in places like Moline and Crawfordsville and Winterset. So we might subtitle this little volume *Selected Short Subjects in Farmers Marketry*.

Nah, let's not. We'll just consider it a loving look at the highlights of a very special phenomenon.

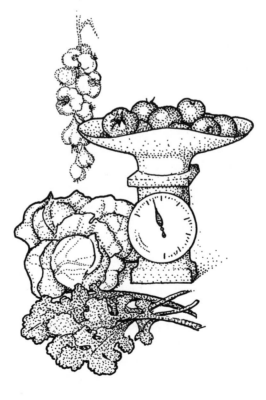

CHAPTER 1

THE FIRST
GLIMMER

It doesn't open with a bang. The arrival of fresh heartland produce at the market place isn't marked by the release of a great torrent of fresh goods, as if there had been an opening of the farm's flood gates. It's more of a trickle.

Just as each farmer plants according to his unique set of conditions, so each market begins on its own schedule, with its own particular collection of early-season vegetables and fruits. And unlike the abundance which will distinguish the market in later weeks, the first crops of the harvest season appear fleetingly, and in smaller amounts. While July will seem to bring the market shopper an endless supply of everything, the markets of late spring yield small-scale treasures: little bundles of tender young asparagus shoots, shiny scarlet stalks of tangy rhubarb, crisp red radishes, and delicate young greens. This is the time to savor the earth's first offerings of the season, probably leaving little in the way of leftovers.

Indeed, many markets don't even open during these early weeks, waiting to unfurl their distinctive shading umbrellas until post-solstice, long after the asparagus has grown woody and the first cuttings of rhubarb gone slippery and limp. But if you can find a market that begins this early, you should seize the chance to enjoy these luscious harvest harbingers.

Asparagus

A welcome sight at winter's end, the first skinny little shoots of asparagus offer the first real sign that the local harvest has begun. When this enigmatic perennial rears its pointy head, we can begin to rid our diets of travel-weary vegetables brought in from the coast, and Florida fruit that couldn't seem to catch a quick enough flight north. Yes, when the asparagus appears, summer's all but under way.

Although asparagus is mentioned in cookbooks dating back to the American Revolution, it remains unclear just when this Eurasian native first arrived on this side of the Atlantic. But for some two centuries now, the green shoots have grown here, both wild among rural fences and under careful cultivation in well-tended plots.

Ripe asparagus is richly green, with closed, compact tips. Spears showing vertical ridges or splayed tips are likely to be old and lacking flavor and tenderness. You also should avoid very dirty asparagus, because it can be just about impossible to get the spears completely clean.

The controversy rages on over the ideal thickness for an asparagus spear. Some people will eat only chopstick-size shoots, while others insist that they've had hot dog-size pieces melt in their mouths. In truth, your best bet lies somewhere in between, at a diameter of about half an inch. Excessively thick or thin stalks often turn out to be tough.

If you do end up with some thick spears in your bunch—and you probably will—don't make the mistake of throwing away the entire lower half. Instead, pare away the tougher sections, gradually cutting deeper as you approach the bottom end. Prepared this way, all of the shoots can be expected to cook in about the same length of time.

In storing the spears, keep in mind that the cut ends provide a channel for the entry and exit of moisture. Keep the ends in water, perhaps standing the spears in a large tumbler, and keep them well chilled to retard the breakdown of the plant's sugars.

A natural diuretic, asparagus provides respectable amounts of vitamins A and C. It adapts itself comfortably to a wide range of preparation methods. You might want to serve perfectly formed, uniformly sized spears quite simply, perhaps steamed and topped with just a drizzle of lemon butter (and please do eat them with your fingers, if you're so inclined). Or you might want to dress them up a bit, with a sauce or in a medley of vegetables. And if they're a day or two too ripe, they'll retire gracefully and delectably as the centerpiece of a kettle of creamy soup.

Asparagus Vinaigrette with Leeks

Serves 4

1 pound fresh asparagus (16–20 shoots)
1 medium leek, trimmed
1 tablespoon white wine vinegar
1 tablespoon fresh lemon juice
1 small clove garlic, minced
½ teaspoon Dijon mustard
½ cup oil (part salad oil, part olive oil)
Pinch of salt
Freshly ground black pepper, to taste
2 hard-boiled eggs, chopped fine
1 tablespoon chopped fresh parsley
Lettuce leaves

Trim the tough ends off the asparagus and peel the thicker stalks. Place in a small amount of water and steam 4–5 minutes or until just barely tender. Remove with tongs to a shallow glass or ceramic dish. Save the steaming liquid.

Split the leek lengthwise and wash carefully. Slice into ¼-inch slices. Blanch for about 3 minutes in the asparagus-steaming liquid. Drain and scatter over the asparagus.

Place the vinegar, lemon juice, mustard, oil, salt, and pepper in a screw-top jar and seal. Shake vigorously for 30 seconds, then pour over the asparagus and leeks. Cover the dish and refrigerate for at least 2 hours.

At serving time, divide the lettuce leaves between four plates. Put four or five asparagus spears, drained, on each plate and sprinkle on some leek slices. Spread the chopped egg over each serving and then sprinkle the chopped parsley over all.

Asparagus Canapes

These tangy appetizers are larger than bite-size, so plan to serve them with a little plate or napkin.

Makes 16

1½ to 2 pounds asparagus (32 shoots)
2 tablespoons butter
½ cup minced onion
1½ tablespoon flour
½ cup milk
8 ounces chilled cream cheese, cut into ½-inch cubes
4 ounces blue cheese
16 slices white bread, crusts removed
½ cup butter, melted

Preheat oven to 375°F.

Cut the asparagus 4 or 5 inches from the tip, peeling the larger stalks and saving the ends for soup, if you like. Stand the tipped spears, cut end down, in a saucepan in one inch of water. Tie them together with a string if necessary. Cover and steam 7–8 minutes or until tender.

Melt the 2 tablespoons butter in a small saucepan. Add the onion and cook until tender. Stir in the flour and cook over medium heat, still stirring, for 2–3 minutes. Add the milk and continue stirring until thickened.

Transfer the white sauce to the top of a double boiler. Add the cream cheese and crumble in the blue cheese. Cook and stir over hot (not boiling) water until cheeses are melted and mixture is thick and fairly smooth.

Using a pastry brush, take a piece of bread and coat both sides with melted butter. Place about 2 tablespoons of the sauce diagonally across the bread and set two asparagus spears on top. Bring the 2 open corners together over the spears and sauce; secure with a toothpick. Repeat with the remaining slices.

Arrange the canapes in a shallow baking dish and heat for 5–7 minutes at 375°F. Serve hot.

Sesame Stir-Fried Asparagus

The two-step cooking procedure allows you to retain the glorious green of the asparagus without having to serve it undercooked.

Serves 6

2 pounds asparagus
1 clove garlic, halved
3 tablespoons peanut oil
½ teaspoon sesame oil
2 tablespoons sesame seeds

Wash the asparagus and slice it diagonally at ½-inch intervals. Separate out the tips and set aside.

Bring a pot of lightly salted water to a boil. Toss in the asparagus slices and cook for about 3 minutes. Remove to a medium-size bowl, using a strainer or slotted spoon. Put the tips into the boiling water and cook for about 60 seconds. Remove and add to the cooked slices.

Set a wok or large skillet over high heat and rub all over with the cut halves of the garlic clove. Discard garlic. Pour the peanut oil into the pan, then add the asparagus. Cook, tossing constantly, for 2–3 minutes, until asparagus is just tender but still crisp and bright green. Sprinkle on the sesame oil and seeds; mix well. Serve hot.

Cream of Asparagus Soup

Rich and creamy, this elegant soup brings new grace to mature asparagus.

Serves 4

1 pound asparagus
1 medium onion, chopped fine
3 tablespoons chopped parsley
3 cups chicken stock
Salt and pepper, to taste
3 tablespoons butter
2 tablespoons flour
Dash of nutmeg
2 egg yolks
½ cup whipping cream
Toasted croutons (optional garnish)

Wash and trim the asparagus. Remove the tips and set aside. Chop the stalks and put them into a kettle with the onion, parsley, and stock. Bring to a boil and simmer, covered, for 10–15 minutes or until the asparagus is tender. Puree the mixture in a blender or food processor, or put it through a food mill. Return the soup to the kettle and season to taste. Set aside.

Melt the butter in a small saucepan; add flour. Stir and cook over medium heat for a minute or two. Return the soup kettle to the burner and add the roux, stirring briskly. Bring soup to a boil, still stirring, then simmer about 5 minutes. Taste. Add a little nutmeg and whatever else you like.

Steam the reserved tips over boiling water until just tender, about 3–4 minutes. Divide the tips between four soup bowls.

Beat the egg yolks and cream. Whisk about ½ cup of the hot soup into the yolk mixture. Return to the soup pot; stir thoroughly. Heat through and serve hot, garnished with croutons if desired.

Rhubarb

Look! There on the ground! It's a fruit! It's a vegetable! No, it's super-weed! Richly foliated and invitingly scarlet, the rhubarb has arrived.

Although we tend to serve it as a fruit, rhubarb actually is a vegetable, a perennial which seems to grow almost everywhere. But despite its appetizing appearance, rhubarb has roots and foliage which are highly toxic, and it's only suitable for eating after it has been cooked.

A respectable source of vitamin C, rhubarb appears at the farmers market early, with later plantings following throughout the summer. It is at peak ripeness when the stalks are firm and crisp and their surface is red or deep pink and shiny. Very thick and very thin pieces should be avoided, as they are often tough and stringy.

While rhubarb is frequently maligned with lots of nose crinkling, its tangy character can bring out the best in the other foods you mix with it. Those who do enjoy the flavor of spring's quasi-fruit might like it prepared most simply: chopped, sweetened with a little brown sugar or honey, and baked for about 30 minutes at 375°F. (To feed it to a baby, use a touch of sugar instead of honey— or no sweetening at all—and thicken it with a little wheat germ or infant cereal if necessary.)

For more particular palates, try using the rhubarb as a featured flavor, mellowing its amiable tang with a mixture of subordinate ingredients.

Grandma's Rhubarb Coffee Cake

This recipe, compliments of my grandmother-in-law, makes a sweet treat for breakfast or teatime. It also works for dessert.

Serves 9

Cake

2 cups flour
½ teaspoon baking soda
½ teaspoon salt
¼ teaspoon cinnamon
Pinch of cloves
Pinch of allspice
7 tablespoons butter or margarine, softened
1¼ cups sugar
2 eggs, beaten
⅓ cup milk
2 cups rhubarb, cut into ½-inch pieces

Topping

⅔ cup flour
½ cup firmly packed brown sugar
¼ cup butter or margarine
¾ cup coconut
¼ cup chopped walnuts

Preheat oven to 350°F. Sift together the flour, soda, salt, and spices. Set aside.

Cream the butter and sugar together and add to the dry mixture along with the eggs and milk. Mix well. Fold in the rhubarb. Turn the mixture into a greased 8-inch square pan.

For the topping, blend the flour, brown sugar, and butter until crumbly. Stir in the nuts and coconut. Sprinkle over the batter.

Bake at 350°F. for 45–50 minutes, until a toothpick inserted in the center comes out clean.

Rhubarb–Banana Bread Pudding

This unusual combination is delicious: sweet, tart, rich, and satisfying.

Serves 6

½ cup unsalted butter, softened
1 cup tightly packed brown sugar, divided
2 eggs
½ teaspoon nutmeg
½ teaspoon vanilla
4 slices Homestyle bread, cubed and toasted
4 cups chopped rhubarb
2 medium bananas, sliced
1 tablespoon fresh lemon juice
1 tablespoon fresh orange juice
2 tablespoons water
Whipped cream

Lightly grease a 2-quart baking dish. Preheat oven to 375°F.

Cream the butter with half of the brown sugar. Beat in the eggs, one at a time, then the nutmeg and vanilla. Fold in the toast cubes.

Spread half of the mixture evenly in the prepared baking dish. Distribute the rhubarb evenly over the batter, and the banana slices over the rhubarb. Sprinkle the remaining sugar over the fruit, then spread on the rest of the bread batter. Mix the liquids together and sprinkle over the top. Bake for 40 minutes at 375°F. Serve warm or at room temperature, topped with whipped cream.

Rhubarb Cheesecake

Were it not for the name, people might never know what makes this dense, rich dessert so fabulous.

Serves 10–12

Crust

1 cup graham-cracker crumbs
⅓ cup unsalted butter, melted
¼ cup sugar

Filling

1 pound rhubarb, trimmed
1⅓ cups sugar, divided
¼ teaspoon salt
Pinch of cinnamon
2 teaspoons cornstarch
2 tablespoons orange juice
2 pounds cream cheese, softened
4 eggs
2 tablespoons flour
1 teaspoon grated orange rind

For the crust, combine the crumbs, butter, and sugar and press mixture into the bottom of a 9-inch springform pan.

Wash the rhubarb well and chop it fine. Put it into a medium saucepan with ⅓ cup of the sugar, the salt, and cinnamon. Cover and cook gently, stirring occasionally, for 8–9 minutes or until tender. Combine the cornstarch and juice; stir into the sauce and cook, stirring constantly, until thickened. Remove from heat; cool.

Preheat oven to 325°F.

In a large bowl, beat the remaining cup of sugar with the cream cheese until fluffy. Beat in the eggs, one at a time, then stir in the flour, orange rind, and ½ cup of the rhubarb sauce (refrigerate the rest of the sauce). Mix well. Turn the mixture into the crumb-bottomed pan. Bake for an hour or so, until the center is set. Turn the heat off and leave the cake in the oven for another hour. Cool and chill several hours or overnight.

At serving time, remove the springform. Slice the cake and serve topped with the reserved rhubarb sauce.

Rhubarbecue Sauce

This smooth, mellow sauce is good on chicken and ribs, but you might also try it atop a burger.

Makes about 1½ cups

½ pound rhubarb, trimmed
½ cup water
⅓ cup brown sugar
2 tablespoons cider vinegar
¼ cup catsup
½ teaspoon dry mustard
½ teaspoon chili powder
3–4 drops Tabasco

Wash rhubarb and chop it fine. Put it into a medium saucepan with the remaining ingredients. Bring to a boil, cover, and simmer gently for 15–20 minutes, until rhubarb is tender. Transfer to a blender or food processor and puree. Chill.

Brush this sauce on grilled meats during the last few minutes of cooking.

Hippity, Hoppity, Summer's On Its Way

As any rabbit can tell you, no single salad is more utterly delectable than the first mélange of summer's early, tender greens. The appearance of tangy leaf lettuces, lively "tops" greens, and those smooth, richly green spinach leaves hails the onset of another season of fresh-from-just-around-the-corner produce.

Included in this most welcome group are the cooking greens: mild beet and collard leaves; the more piquant dandelion, turnip, and mustard greens; kale, spinach, Swiss chard, and broccoli leaves. An excellent source of calcium, these greens can be enjoyed on their own, steamed or sautéed, or mixed into hot soups, casseroles, or stews.

Then there are the greens almost certainly bound for the salad bowl. These are many, encompassing romaine, buttercrunch, escarole, Bibb, Boston, and the looseleaf lettuces, as well as the intriguing flavors of arugula, radicchio, endive, chicory, and watercress: a veritable garden-invader's dream come true.

When shopping for greens, remember that biggest is not necessarily best. Choose leafy goods that are firm and springy in texture. Heads that are heavy for their size tend to be a better buy. Best left on the farmer's table are heads with yellowing, limp, or brown-edged leaves, which probably have been around a bit too long. Greens with coarse, fibrous stems also should be avoided. And of course, leaves showing insect holes tell you that somebody has already gotten dibs on that piece.

Many of these broad-leaved goodies are wonderful just tossed together in a bowl, with a light and luscious coating of simple vinaigrette. If you do opt for salad, try to start several hours in advance of serving time. Wash the greens extra carefully, using numerous sinkloads of tepid water. Then spin off or shake out as much water as you can, roll up the greens in a tea towel and chill them for a while. This will crispen the leaves, improving considerably the texture of your salad.

When it's time to assemble the salad, tear the leaves up by hand—cutting can bruise and discolor them. Wait until the very last minute to add the dressing, to avoid a limp, soggy mixture. And please, please use dressing sparingly—overdressing salad is among the most common culinary crimes.

Because the ingredients in your salad include some of the very best produce available to you, try to choose a variety of dressing which will complement the mixture, not overpower it. If it's the dressing you wish to showcase, chop up a head of supermarket iceberg and coat it with the stuff. Adulterating good greens with a domineering dressing is a flagrant waste of natural resources!

As for cooked greens, you should start out, again, with exhaustive rinsing. The crunch of grit can douse the flames under a full-roaring appetite with instant finality. Boiling or steaming greens in a well-flavored meat or vegetable stock will enhance their flavor, and the sharpest-tasting ones, such as turnip leaves and mustard greens, can be nicely neutralized by cooking in a little cream or butter, or both.

But it is in *cooking* greens that you lose some of the bargain. Spinach weighs in at 80 to 90 percent water. A huge mound of crisp leaves can be reduced to a mere serving or two with just a quick steaming. So be sure to buy enough greens for cooking.

Of course, if you get carried away at the market, there are lots of things you can do with your new jungle of greenery. And if you've let the whole load sit around a day or two too long, there are solutions for that, too. Here are some suggestions for making it all disappear.

Know When To Put a Lid On It

Vegetables and water are a natural pair. From seedling to dinner dish, fresh produce relies on water for germination, nourishment, cleanliness, and finally, cooking. But what's the best way to use water in cooking your vegetables? Steam? A boiling-water bath? A gentle poaching? An uncovered simmer?

Well, I have no hard and fast rules to offer—save for one. My grandmother, a gracious and diminutive woman who had a special way with vegetables, said that if a vegetable grows above ground, it should be cooked uncovered. If it grows under the dirt, put a lid on it.

If it was good enough for Gramma Chick, it's good enough for me.

Braised Beet Greens with Almonds

This dish also can be made with collard, dandelion, or broccoli greens.

Serves 2

2 tablespoons butter
1 small clove garlic, minced
½ pound beet greens, deveined, well washed, and dried
⅓ cup milk
¼ cup sliced almonds, toasted

Chop greens coarsely and set aside. Melt the butter in a large skillet. Sauté the garlic briefly, then stir in the greens and continue sautéeing until they begin to wilt. Add the milk, cover, and cook a few minutes, until the greens are tender. Uncover and continue cooking until the liquid evaporates. Serve hot, sprinkled with almonds.

Kale-Stuffed Calzone

This hearty, wholesome pastry makes good use of a mound of kale.

Serves 8

Dough

1 package (1 tablespoon) active dry yeast
1 tablespoon honey
1 cup lukewarm water
1½ teaspoons salt
2 cups whole-wheat flour
1–1½ cups unbleached white flour

Filling

1½ pound kale
2 tablespoons butter
½ cup minced onion
2 cloves garlic, minced
1 15-ounce carton ricotta cheese (a scant pound)
8 ounces mozzarella cheese, shredded
1 egg, lightly beaten
8 ounces prosciutto, chopped
½ tablespoon rosemary
Salt and pepper

Combine the yeast, honey, and water. Let sit until foamy, about 3–5 minutes. Gradually stir in the whole-wheat flour, the salt, and enough white flour to make a soft dough. Turn out onto a floured board and knead until smooth and elastic, about 10 minutes. Let rise until doubled, about 45–60 minutes. Meanwhile, assemble the filling.

Wash the kale carefully. Pull out the middle vein and place the leaves in a large kettle. Cook them in the water that clings to them just until they wilt, about 2–3 minutes. Chop the kale fine and set it aside.

Melt the butter in a large skillet and sauté the onion and garlic until tender. Stir in the kale and sauté another couple of minutes. Remove from heat.

In a large bowl, combine the ricotta, mozzarella, egg, rosemary, salt, and pepper. Mix well and add the kale mixture and the prosciutto. Blend thoroughly.

Preheat the oven to 400°F.

Punch the dough down. Using a pastry scraper or a dull knife, divide the dough into eight equal parts. Roll each portion into an oval about ⅛ inch thick. Divide the filling evenly among the dough pieces, piling it on half of each oval. Fold the empty half of the dough over the filling and seal with the tines of a fork. Poke a few fork holes in the top of each pastry to allow the steam to escape. Bake the calzones at 400°F for 20–25 minutes, until they are golden brown. Brush the pastries with a little melted butter and serve them hot.

Rice Salad Florentine

This refreshing salad can appear as a side dish or as head billing for supper.

Serves 6

3 cups freshly cooked rice
⅓ cup olive oil
2 tablespoons white wine vinegar
1 tablespoon fresh lemon juice
½ teaspoon sugar
Salt and pepper to taste
½ pound spinach, washed and chopped
½ cup chopped celery
½ cup sliced scallions
2 tablespoons finely chopped fresh basil
4 slices bacon, fried crisp

While the rice is cooking, make the dressing by whisking together the olive oil, vinegar, lemon juice, sugar, salt, and pepper. Drizzle over the rice while it is still warm and chill for at least 2 or 3 hours.

Gently blend in the spinach, celery, scallions, and basil. Serve at room temperature, with bacon crumbled over the top.

Spinach Quiche

This is a special pie, with a tangy whole-wheat–cheese crust and a creamy filling.

Serves 6

Crust

1 cup whole-wheat pastry flour
½ cup freshly grated Parmesan cheese
½ teaspoon salt
3 tablespoons cold butter, cut into pieces
3 tablespoons oil
2 tablespoons cold water

Filling

½ pound spinach
1 tablespoon butter
½ medium onion, chopped
1 medium clove garlic, chopped fine
Salt to taste
4–5 ounces Gruyère or other Swiss cheese, shredded
1 cup half & half
2 eggs
½ teaspoon dry mustard
¼ teaspoon nutmeg

Preheat the oven to 425°F.

Crust

Mix the flour, cheese, and salt together. Cut in the butter, using a pastry cutter or two knives, until the mixture has the consistency of coarse crumbs. Whisk together the oil and water with a fork and quickly dribble it into the flour mixture, tossing with the fork. Gather the dough into a ball, wrap it in plastic and chill for 30 minutes or so. Roll it out to fit a 9- or 10-inch pie plate and gently place it in the pan. Prick the dough in several places with a fork and bake it for 7 or 8 minutes, just until it begins to take on a little color. Let cool.

Filling

First wash and chop the spinach. Cook it in just the water clinging to it until it wilts, about 2 minutes. Remove the spinach from the pan using a slotted spoon and place it on paper towels. Squeeze out the moisture and set it aside. Melt the butter in a medium skillet and sauté the onion and garlic until just tender. Add the spinach and salt and sauté the mixture another minute or so. Remove from the heat and set aside. Sprinkle the cheese over the surface of the prebaked crust. Spread the spinach mixture over it. Beat together the half & half, eggs, mustard, and nutmeg. Pour the mixture evenly over the spinach.

Bake the pie for 10 minutes at 425°F, then reduce the oven temperature to 375°F and bake 15–20 minutes longer, until the surface is set and golden brown. Serve warm or at room temperature.

Cream of Spinach and Basil Soup

A rich, flavorful, and filling cold soup.

Serves 4

6 small redskin potatoes
1 cup chopped onion
3 tablespoons butter
1 cup chopped spinach, packed firm
½ cup minced basil, packed firm
1 cup well-flavored chicken stock
2 tablespoons chopped parsley
½ teaspoon salt
Pinch of white pepper
1 cup whipping cream

Place the potatoes in a medium saucepan and cover with cold water. Bring to a boil and cook about 15 minutes or until very tender. Cool slightly and pull off skins. Cut into large chunks and set aside.

Sauté onion in butter until soft. Add the spinach and basil and stir for 1 minute. Stir in the stock, potatoes, parsley, salt, and pepper; simmer over very low heat for 10 minutes.

Cool the mixture slightly and puree it in a blender or food processor. Transfer to a large bowl.

Stir in the cream. Chill the soup thoroughly. At serving time, taste carefully and if necessary, adjust seasonings. Thin the soup with a little milk if desired.

Easier Caesar Salad

Wars have been waged over the best way to make the classic salad born in Tijuana. I like this simple approach. Anchovies somehow seem more appetizing when they are in a tube.

Serves 4

1 medium head romaine lettuce
½ loaf day-old French bread
1 clove garlic, cut in half
1 tablespoon olive oil
Creamy Caesar dressing (recipe follows)
⅓ cup freshly grated Parmesan cheese

Wash the romaine leaves and pull out the middle veins. Tear the leaves into large pieces and roll up in paper or cotton towels; chill.

Cut the bread into ½-inch cubes. Heat a medium-size skillet and rub the inside surface with the cut garlic clove. Discard garlic. Heat the olive oil in the skillet, add the bread cubes, and toss until golden. Drain on paper towels.

Toss the lettuce with the dressing until it is evenly coated. Add the Parmesan cheese, toss gently, then spread the croutons over the top.

Creamy Caesar Dressing

1 egg yolk
½ cup olive oil
2 tablespoons wine vinegar
2 tablespoons fresh lemon juice
1 medium clove garlic, minced
½ teaspoon anchovy paste
A pinch of dry mustard
Lots of freshly ground black pepper

Beat the egg yolk in a small bowl with a fork or small whisk. Add the oil in a thin, steady stream, beating until smooth and uniform. Whisk in the vinegar and lemon juice, mixing well, then add the remaining ingredients. Blend thoroughly and chill.

Cream of Lettuce Soup

Unusual and intriguing, this soup gives new purpose to the excessive lettuce supply you may have picked up at the market.

Serves 6

2 cups chicken stock
½ teaspoon thyme
12 cups torn leaf lettuce
2 tablespoons butter
3 tablespoons chopped red onion
2 tablespoons flour
Pinch of salt and white pepper
1 cup half & half
Plain yogurt
Snipped chives

Combine the stock and thyme in a large kettle. Add the lettuce and cook gently until wilted. Transfer the mixture to a blender or food processor and puree. Set aside.

Rinse out the kettle and wipe dry. Melt the butter in it and stir in the onion. Sauté gently until softened. Mix in the flour, salt, and pepper and cook for a minute or two. Stir in half & half; cook and stir until smooth. Add the spinach mixture and blend well. Pour the mixture into a serving bowl; chill.

Serve the soup cold, topped with a tablespoon or so of yogurt and a sprinkling of chives.

Under the Surface

With all of that horticultural hoopla going on at the soil's surface, it's difficult to imagine that all is quiet down where the sun doesn't shine. Indeed not. In fact, some of the farmer's very tastiest morsels appear during summer's early weeks, as many crops achieve a delectable state of incipient ripeness. With the passing of just a few sunsets, this delicate perfection will be lost in the later flood of the season's more robust flavors. These are the weeks of tender, downsized beets; mild and crispy palatable radishes; sweet carrots, no bigger than a baby's pinky; and the debut of the Pungent Family: the chives, scallions, and leeks.

In all of these subterraneans, look for firm, nonslippery roots, free of blemishes. The neck ends should be neither thick and woody, which suggests overaging, nor soft, which can signal decay. The top growth should be crisp and green, and the "meat" of the vegetable intensely hued, be it fluorescent orange, rain-forest green or—you guessed it—beet red.

Leeks and Peas with Orange Vinaigrette

My friend Beth and her dad worked up this one. It's simple and elegant, a real feast of contrasting flavors in glorious Technicolor.

Serves 6

4 leeks
1 pound fresh sweet peas

Dressing

3 large navel oranges, peeled, sliced crosswise, and chilled

Orange Vinaigrette

⅓ cup safflower oil
2 tablespoons red wine vinegar
2 tablespoons orange juice
Basil, thyme, marjoram, and fresh-ground pepper to taste
Bibb lettuce leaves

Wash the leeks carefully and cut into rings, including some of the green part. Blanch in boiling water until just tender, about 1½–2 minutes. Drain well and place in a large bowl.

Shuck the peas and steam over boiling water until just barely tender, about 3–4 minutes. Place in the bowl with the blanched leeks.

Make the dressing by combining all the ingredients in a jar. Cover and shake well. Drizzle a little of the dressing over the leek-pea mixture and chill both the vegetables and the dressing.

At serving time, arrange lettuce leaves on six salad plates. Fan the orange slices evenly over the lettuce leaves. Scatter the leek-pea mixture over the oranges and drizzle on a little more dressing.

Curried Vichyssoise with Apple

The classic goes adventurous with this soup, a delightful mixture of flavors and textures. The quantity of curry is left variable, depending on your preference.

Serves 6 (as a first course)

3 medium leeks
1 medium onion
3 medium potatoes
¼ cup butter
½–1 teaspoon curry powder
3 cups chicken stock
Salt and white pepper
Pinch of mace
1½ cups whipping cream
1 medium-size Granny Smith apple
2 tablespoons snipped chives

Wash and slice the leeks thin, then wash them again. Peel and slice the onion and potatoes thin. Melt the butter in a kettle; add the vegetables and curry powder. Toss to coat. Cover the kettle and cook over low heat until vegetables are tender. Add stock, salt, white pepper, and mace; simmer for 20 minutes.

Cool the the soup slightly and puree in a blender or food processor. Finish cooling, then add cream. Chill.

At serving time, adjust seasonings if desired. Pour the soup into individual bowls. Core and peel the apple; grate it and toss in the chives. Sprinkle a tablespoon or two of the mixture over each bowl as you serve.

Baked Baby Beets

A far cry from anything sold in a jar, these beets are sweet, tender, and utterly luscious. If you think you don't like beets, try this dish.

Serves 3–4

15–20 baby (1-inch diameter) beets, trimmed
1 medium onion, chopped coarse
½ cup hot chicken stock or water
Salt and fresh ground pepper
2 tablespoons cold butter

Preheat the oven to 350°F.

Scrub the beets and slice thin. Place in a small greased baking dish in alternating layers with the onion. Carefully pour on the stock; season with salt and pepper. Dot with slivers of butter. Cover and bake at 350°F for 30–40 minutes, until beets are tender.

Spring Radish Spread

Zesty and appetizing, this mixture also can be spread in a pita, maybe coupled with some alfalfa sprouts or crisp lettuce, for a quick sandwich.

Makes about 2 cups

1 8-ounce package cream cheese, softened
1–2 tablespoons prepared horseradish, drained
1 tablespoon chopped chives or green onion tops
1 teaspoon fresh dill, chopped
½ teaspoon salt
1 cup finely chopped red radishes
Crackers or French bread

In a medium bowl, mix cream cheese, horseradish, chives, dill, salt, and radishes. Cover and refrigerate until serving time, at least 1–2 hours. Serve atop crackers or slices of crusty French bread.

Mustard-Glazed Baby Carrots

Choose your favorite mustard for this beautiful side dish.

Serves 6

1½ pound baby carrots
¼ cup butter
3 tablespoons prepared mustard
½ cup mild honey
Salt and fresh ground pepper to taste
Chopped parsley

Scrub the carrots well; it shouldn't be necessary to peel them, though you can if you prefer. Steam over hot water until barely tender, about 4–6 minutes.

In a medium saucepan, combine the butter, mustard, and honey. Heat, stirring constantly, over medium heat for about 3 minutes. Season to taste; stir in carrots. Garnish with parsley and serve hot.

To Peel Or Not To Peel?

In the final analysis, leaving the skins on your vegetables or taking them off is a personal choice. Some people prefer to eat them, opting for the added texture and roughage they provide. But the skins aren't where the vitamins are. Contrary to popular myth, the heaviest concentration of a vegetable's nutrients isn't in the skin, but rather just beneath it. So it does make sense to cook things like potatoes in their skins, slipping them off after they're done. If you do like to leave the skins on things like carrots, potatoes, beets, and turnips, it's wise to have a dependable vegetable brush on hand. I like to use those ball-shaped woven plastic dish-scrubbing pads for cleaning vegetables. They can help remove all the grit without damaging the vegetable's skin, and when they're finished they'll go obediently into the dishwasher for cleaning.

CHAPTER 2

FRESH INFUSIONS

AN HERBAL PERSPECTIVE

Somewhere along the line, in the relentless advance of technology which has brought us things like freeze-dried shallots and powdered spinach, the use of fresh herbs has withered nearly into the status of a lost art. No longer found in every garden and hanging, inverted, from the rafters of every pantry, herbs have come to be recognized by the compact metal boxes and little labeled jars in which they are packed for supermarket sale. A pity, really.

For while sometimes dried herbs are adequate for use in soups and casseroles and with meats, seldom is the dried version really preferable to fresh. Particularly in the summer, when all of your produce is as fresh as fresh can be, it's worth the extra trouble to buy, wash, and mince the real thing into your carefully prepared dishes.

Although few people go to the farmers market just for herbs, a large-scale farmer usually brings a few sprigs of this and that with his collection of other produce. Often a fresh herbalist, dealing exclusively in the tasty green seasonings, appears as a market merchant. Sometimes it's even an earthy, vaguely mystical "herb lady." At any rate, no self-respecting discussion of the farmers market would be complete without a few words devoted to the allure of herbs.

Another of the early season's delectable virtues, fresh herbs appear by the fragrant bundle, nestled in alongside tender greens and baby vegetables. In shopping for them, look for bright green, resilient foliage. To gauge their flavor, try gently bruising a leaf or two with a thumbnail, then whiff. But be gentle and discreet— the farmer isn't likely to appreciate being left with piles of mangled greenery.

Once home, store the herbs in the refrigerator in ventilated plastic bags. As with other leafy greens, you should put off washing herbs until just before you use them.

Most herbs should be minced rather finely before being added to recipes. Basil sometimes is used in mere shreds—or even whole, as an intriguing salad ingredient. But usually the herb should subtly permeate the entire mixture.

In general, you should triple the amounts listed for dried herbs in recipes. But because no two sprigs of tarragon taste exactly the same—and, more important, no two people have the same tastes—it makes sense to let your own good judgment be your guide. Be creative, imaginative, maybe even a little reckless: the potential for blending fresh herbs into exciting combinations is bounded only loosely by your imagination.

But if you would like a starting point, here are some of the herbs found most often in outdoor markets, and some of the foods folks most often have found them compatible with.

Basil: beef, pork, lamb, and seafoods; cheese; vegetables; eggs; in soups, salads, and breads

Bay (leaves): beef, lamb, poultry, and seafoods; vegetables; eggs; in soups and desserts

Chervil: beef, fish; vegetables; eggs; cheese; in soups

Cilantro (fresh coriander, also called Mexican or Chinese parsley): pork; cheese; vegetables; fruit; in soups, breads, and uncooked sauces

Dill: with all kinds of meat; eggs; cheese; vegetables; in soups and desserts

Fennel: pork, cheese and eggs; in breads and desserts

Marjoram: beef, pork, lamb, and shellfish; eggs; vegetables; in soups and breads

Mint: lamb; vegetables; cheese; fruit

Oregano: beef, lamb, poultry, and shellfish; eggs; vegetables; in soups and breads

Parsley: beef, poultry; eggs; vegetables; cheese; in soups, salads, and breads

Rosemary: with all kinds of meat; eggs; vegetables; in soups

Sage: pork, poultry, and fish; cheese; vegetables; in soups

Savory: with all kinds of meat; eggs; vegetables; in soups and breads

Sorrel: beef, pork, poultry and fish; eggs; cheese; in soups and salads

Tarragon (French): poultry and seafood; cheese; eggs; vegetables; in soups

Thyme: with all kinds of meat; cheese; eggs, and vegetables; in soups and breads

If Only You Could Bottle It

One of the best ways to preserve the flavor of fresh herbs—better than drying or freezing them—is to turn them into vinegar. For the small amount of effort involved, you are doubly rewarded. Not only do you get a bottle of versatile, imaginatively flavored vinegar, terrific as a gift item, you also can enjoy the herb itself, months after it appeared on the farmer's table, with very little loss of flavor. Just take it out of the vinegar, blot it dry, and chop it up.

To make herb vinegar, use clean glass bottles with nonmetal caps, to avoid an off-flavored reaction. Put whole sprigs of herbs into the bottles, or use just the leaves. Cover them with a good vinegar, cap, label, and store the bottles for at least a month before using.

When the steeping period ends, you might want to divide the vinegar into smaller bottles for more convenient use. Adding a small, fresh sprig of the featured herb is a nice touch.

Almost any culinary herb can be used in vinegar, but some perennial favorites include basil, dill, rosemary, sage, tarragon, and thyme. Use a couple in combination, if you like, pairing a strong, assertive herb with a milder one.

Pesto Potential

Pesto, the rich green condiment made from basil, garlic, and cheese, is a full-flavored and wonderfully versatile meal maker. Long loved as a coating for pasta, its uses go way beyond noodles. And the more you use pesto, the more ideas you'll come up with for using it. What a happy cycle!

Try spreading a thin layer of pesto onto pizza dough before smearing on the tomato sauce—or skip the red stuff altogether. The fat in the cheese and the olive oil will form a kind of barrier between dough and toppings, warding off the danger of ending up with a soggy crust.

You can use pesto as the featured flavor in calzones, cannelloni, or manicotti, blending it into the ricotta-cheese filling mixtures. Or slip it in between the savory layers of your favorite lasagne.

It also can be used to liven up a dish of rice, tossed in with a fork shortly before serving. Or tuck it into the middle of an omelette, or stir it into the mayonnaise bound for your best salad or sandwich combination.

You might like to try it on a sandwich with homemade bread and thick slabs of ripe tomato, or maybe swirled across the top of a platter of Fettucine Alfredo.

OK, now it's your turn.

Cream of Sorrel Soup

This rich, elegant soup is an invention of a woman named Waneta Biernacki. Waneta and her husband, Ted, travel to farmers markets around Chicago, selling the potted herbs and other plants that they grow year-round in their greenhouse.

Serves 6–8

1 large red potato, peeled and diced
5 cups chicken broth
1½ cups sorrel
4 tablespoons fresh chervil (or 4 teaspoons dried)
2 shallots
4 ounces butter
1 cup half & half
2 egg yolks
Herb-flavored croutons

Cook the potato gently in chicken broth until tender. Chop sorrel, chervil, and shallots fine and sauté in butter for 3–4 minutes. Add to the broth mixture and cook gently for 10 minutes longer. Beat the cream and egg yolks together and add to the soup, stirring until slightly thickened. Blend in blender until smooth. Heat gently and serve hot with herb-flavored croutons.

Fresh Herb Biscuits

If you absolutely cannot find fresh oregano or basil, substitute one-third as much dried herb. But please, don't use dried parsley.

Makes about 28 biscuits

1 cup unbleached white flour
1 cup whole-wheat flour
1 tablespoon baking powder
2 teaspoons sugar
½ teaspoon salt
2 teaspoons minced fresh oregano
1 teaspoon minced fresh basil
6 tablespoons unsalted butter, chilled
⅔ cup cold milk
2 teaspoons Dijon mustard
3 scallions, sliced (include some green part)
2 tablespoons minced fresh parsley
1 medium clove garlic, minced

Preheat oven to 425°F.

Mix flours, baking powder, sugar, salt, oregano, and basil in a large bowl. Cut in the butter with a pastry blender or two knives, working the mixture until it resembles coarse crumbs. Combine the milk and mustard in a small bowl; stir in the scallions, parsley, and garlic. Pour it over the flour-butter mixture and toss with a fork just until all the ingredients are moistened.

Pat the dough out on a well-floured board, to a thickness of ½ inch. Cut into rounds, using a well-floured biscuit cutter or drinking glass. Place the rounds on a lightly greased baking sheet. Bake at 425°F for 15–20 minutes or until golden. Serve warm, slathered with butter.

Dill Soup

Allow plenty of time for this savory, summery soup to chill before you serve it.

Serves 6

1 quart chicken or vegetable stock
1 large potato, chopped
1 small onion, chopped
1 medium cucumber
2 cups milk
¾ cup sour cream
½ cup chopped fresh dill weed
Salt and pepper

Put the stock, potato, and onion into a saucepan and bring to a boil. Simmer until the potato is tender. Cool to room temperature.

Meanwhile, peel the cucumber and halve it lengthwise. Scoop out the seeds and cut the cucumber into large chunks.

Puree the cooled soup in a blender or food processor, adding the cucumber pieces gradually, until the mixture is very smooth.

Transfer the mixture to a large serving bowl. Whisk in the milk, then the sour cream. Add the dill weed and season to taste.

Chill thoroughly. Readjust the seasonings before serving, if necessary.

Garnish each serving with snipped chives or scallion greens, or with thin slices of cucumber.

Fresh Herb Cream

This delicious dip is just the thing for all the glorious vegetables you bought at the farmers market to serve on a crudité platter. Substitute dried herbs only where you really must.

Makes about 1¾ cups

⅓ cup heavy cream, well chilled
⅓ cup basil leaves, well chopped
¼ cup chopped chervil or parsley
⅓ cup snipped chives
1 teaspoon chopped thyme leaves
1 large egg
1 tablespoon fresh lemon juice
1 tablespoon white wine vinegar
2 teaspoons Dijon mustard
½ teaspoon salt
A few grains of cayenne pepper
Freshly ground black pepper
1 cup high-quality vegetable oil

In a medium-size bowl, combine the cream with the basil, chervil, chives, and thyme. Chill.

Place the egg, lemon juice, vinegar, mustard, salt, cayenne, and pepper in a blender jar. Turn the motor on low and add the oil in a thin, steady stream. Turn off the motor when the mixture is slightly thickened.

Fold the mayonnaise mixture into the herbed cream, using a rubber spatula. Cover and chill several hours or overnight. Let the mixture sit at room temperature for 30 minutes before serving.

Processor Pesto al Pecan

After playing around with pesto combinations for a while, I've concluded that you really have to use the kind of cheese that costs about twice as much as it should. Be sure your nuts are fresh and your oil top quality, too. Good pesto involves a certain measure of commitment.

Makes about 2 cups

2 cups packed fresh basil leaves
3 cloves garlic, chopped
4 ounces toasted chopped pecans
1 cup freshly grated Parmesan cheese
½ cup olive oil
Salt and fresh ground pepper

Put the basil in a food processor fitted with the metal blade. Process with on-off turns, scraping the bowl as needed, until chopped fine. Add the garlic and pecans and mix until minced in. Sprinkle the cheese around and mix in. Scrape down the sides of the work bowl again, then turn on the motor and pour the olive oil down the feed tube in a thin, steady stream. Stop the motor when the pesto is thoroughly mixed.

If you're not using the pesto right away, put it in a suitably sized container and put plastic wrap directly on its surface to prevent undue darkening.

Blender Bernaise Sauce

This is sublime on top of a freshly grilled steak, but it also works with other meats and with vegetables.

Makes about ¾ cup

3 egg yolks
¼ cup vinegar
¼ cup dry white wine
1 tablespoon chopped shallots
2 teaspoons chopped fresh tarragon
¼ teaspoon salt
⅛ teaspoon freshly ground pepper
½ cup butter

Put the yolks in a blender jar and blend briefly. Combine the vinegar, wine, shallots, tarragon, salt, and pepper in a small saucepan and cook until the mixture is reduced to 2 tablespoons. Cool to lukewarm, then add to the yolks.

Wipe out the little pan and melt the butter in it. When the butter is bubbly, turn on the blender and pour it in—in a thin, steady stream, just until the sauce is of the thickness you like. Turn the motor off, transfer the sauce to an attractive vessel of some sort and serve immediately.

Routissons

The fresh herbs really define this French pork stew—a classic.

Serves 6–8

3 pounds lean, boneless pork, cut into 2-inch cubes
2 teaspoons chopped fresh marjoram
2 teaspoons chopped fresh thyme
1 whole sage leaf, chopped, or a pinch of rubbed sage
1 clove garlic, minced
¼ cup vegetable and/or olive oil
Salt and pepper
½ cup red wine vinegar
½ teaspoon grated lemon peel
½ cup minced fresh parsley
2 tablespoons chopped fresh basil
2 tablespoons snipped chives or minced green onion tops
Hot cooked rice

Wipe the meat dry with paper toweling and sprinkle with the marjoram, thyme, sage, and garlic. Let stand for an hour.

Heat the oil in a large, heavy skillet or dutch oven. Add the meat and cook, stirring often, over medium heat until it is quite brown and crisp. This may take as long as 30 minutes. Season with salt and pepper to taste.

Drain the fat from the skillet. Stir in vinegar, scraping up any cooked-on bits from the bottom and sides of the pan. Cover and simmer over low heat until the meat is tender, about 40–50 minutes. If the meat begins to dry out as it cooks, sprinkle on a little water or dry red wine.

At serving time, skim off any excess fat. Stir in the lemon peel, parsley, basil, and chives. Serve immediately, with hot cooked rice.

CHAPTER 3

THE GREENIES

A CABBAGE CLAN

Broccoli, Cauliflower, Cabbage, Brussels Sprouts

There are vegetables, and then there are *vegetables*.

Some are light and delicate, even sweet: young peas, tender squashes, bright and crunchy baby carrots.

And some are serious veggies. When Mom told you to eat yours, she meant these. Stout, sturdy, and flavorfully assertive, these species hail from the land of cabbage, a place where youngsters are forever being told to put their best head forward or to turn over a new leaf. Yes, these are true vegetable's vegetables.

Members of the cabbage family are a varied lot, but they also share some rather endearing common traits. The budding varieties, broccoli and cauliflower, can appear as early as the end of June, while solid cabbage, bok choy (Chinese cabbage), and brussels sprouts tend to hang back in favor of a more fashionably late entrance.

But like other good relatives, the Greenies all are at their best when they first arrive at your house. After a few days they begin to lose their crisp tastiness and may even take on a bit of a foul odor. (When other kinds of family members begin to strain the threads on your welcome mat it's not uncommon for the Greenies to do the same thing.)

In buying solid-cored savoy and other spherical cabbages, look for firm, hard heads that seem heavy for their size. Outer leaves should be free of serious blemishes and resplendent in their intended color—red or green. Wilted or discolored outer leaves signal overaging, as do leaf stems which are separated from the base. And if there's a worm hole on the outermost leaf, chances are he's still residing within—or at least has tunneled out his calling card.

Brussels sprouts, essentially baby cabbages (how chic!) are at their best when the outer leaves are tight and bright green. Wilted or ragged leaves and those with lots of holes in them suggest worm damage and should be left behind. A smudgy, dirty appearance can be a clue to the presence of lice.

Try to find small sprouts, all of roughly equal size, so they will cook evenly. And steer clear of sprouts that are puffy, because they probably are of low quality.

As for the flower heads—cauliflower and broccoli—keep your eye out for compact, tightly clustered buds atop crisp, firm stalks. Avoid pieces with soft, mushy, or discolored spots on the heads. Very dirty or speckled-looking cauliflower may have sustained insect damage, mold growth, or decay. Broccoli with very thick or woody stems or open cores at the base may be tough, although you can sometimes pare away the base of the stalk to reveal a reasonably tender and tasty center.

All of the cabbage kin are tasty items eaten fresh, or lightly cooked, with a sauce or in a conglomeration of other vegetables. But one of this family's greatest virtues is its plain good looks. If these vegetables were to get together and send out a Christmas card, every year it would be the one that arrived earliest, impeccably lettered, and depicting the uniformly handsome clan, each member perfectly formed and radiant in its seasonal hue. A true success story.

The cabbages, either red or green, make terrific bowls. Simply take a slice off the bottom so it will sit solidly, hollow out the head with a sharp paring knife, and fill it with a dip, sauce, salad, cold soup, or whatever strikes your fancy.

And almost any crudité platter can be beautified with the addition of a few cauliflower buds, broccoli florets, or raw sliced brussels sprouts. It's a bountiful palette from which to work; let your imagination run free.

Broccoli Salad

This is an excellent way to enjoy a head of broccoli on a hot summer day. Take care not to overcook the broccoli; you want to experience its crunch.

Serves 4–5

1 medium-size head broccoli
½ cup sliced green pimiento olives
¼ cup chopped red onion
3 hard-boiled eggs, chopped coarse
2 teaspoons chopped fresh dill weed
⅓ cup mayonnaise
Salt and pepper

Cut the broccoli into bit-size florets. Chop a few of the thinner stalks, too (save the heavy trunks for soup). Immerse the broccoli in boiling water for 60 seconds; plunge into a bowl of ice water to arrest the cooking process.

When cooled, remove the broccoli from the water and blot dry. Combine it with the rest of the ingredients; mix thoroughly.

Chill well before serving.

Broccoli-Corn Salad

A colorful mixture, this salad puts leftover corn to good use.

Serves 4

2 cups broccoli florets
1 heaping cup cooked corn kernels (2 medium ears)
¼ cup finely chopped red bell pepper
2 medium scallions, sliced
3 tablespoons rice wine vinegar
1½ tablespoons vegetable oil
A pinch each of: salt, pepper, cumin, chili powder, and oregano

Bring about a quart of water to a boil in a medium-size saucepan. Drop in the broccoli; cook for about 60 seconds. Drain. Toss with the corn, bell pepper, and scallions.

In a small jar, combine the remaining ingredients. Cover and shake. Drizzle over the vegetables; chill thoroughly. Serve cold.

Cauliflower Pie

A real treat, this special savory pie explodes with flavors and is long on eye appeal to boot.

Serves 6

Crust

3 medium russet potatoes
2 tablespoons minced onion
½ teaspoon salt

Filling

1 large-ish head cauliflower
2 tablespoons butter
1 cup chopped onion
2–3 cloves garlic, minced
1 tablespoon chopped fresh basil
Salt and pepper
1 egg, beaten
4–6 ounces sharp Cheddar cheese
2 tablespoons fine, dry bread crumbs
Paprika

Preheat the oven to 375°F.

Parboil the potatoes in their skins for 10 minutes. Cool until easy to handle, then peel and shred. Mix in the onion and salt; pat the mixture into a buttered 9-inch pie plate, extending the rim slightly above the edge of the pan. Bake for 30 minutes.

Meanwhile, separate the cauliflower into small florets and set over boiling water in a steamer. After 10 minutes, remove half of the florets and set them aside. Continue steaming the remainder for 20 minutes more, or until very tender. Put into a medium bowl and mash with a fork or a potato masher.

Melt the butter in a large skillet. Sauté onions and garlic gently until tender. Mix in the basil, salt, and pepper, then the mashed cauliflower. Sauté for another minute or so. Remove from heat and stir in the egg.

To assemble the pie, scatter a third of the cheese over the potato crust. Spread the mashed cauliflower mixture evenly over it, then another third of the cheese. Spread the steamed florets over the cheese, arranging them so the heads are up. Sprinkle on the rest of the cheese, then the bread crumbs, then a little paprika. Bake at 375°F for 30–35 minutes. Serve warm or at room temperature.

Creamy Cauliflower-Cheese Soup

Serves 6

3 cups water
1 medium onion, chopped fine
1 teaspoon salt
¼ teaspoon pepper
Florets from one medium cauliflower, cut into uniform sizes
2 tablespoons butter
2 tablespoons flour
1 cup heated chicken stock
2 cups milk
4 ounces sharp Cheddar cheese, shredded (about 1 cup)
2 tablespoons chopped basil

In a heavy 4-quart kettle, combine the water, onion, salt, and pepper. Cover and warm over medium heat for 5 minutes. Then add the cauliflower and cook, covered, for 15 minutes more or until cauliflower is tender.

In a small saucepan, melt the butter, then add the flour and cook for a minute or two, until lightly colored. Slowly stir in the stock and whisk until smooth. Add to the soup pot, mixing well.

Heat the milk in the same saucepan, then add the cheese. Stir until the cheese melts, then add this mixture to the soup pot, along with the basil. Mix well and heat gently until piping hot.

Quick Slaw McGraw
(a food processor tale)

This slaw is easy and refreshing.

Serves 6

½ medium green cabbage (about a pound)
½ pound carrots (3–4 medium)
½ medium red onion
1 cup mayonnaise
1 tablespoon fresh lemon juice
2 teaspoons Dijon mustard
Pinch of sugar
Salt and pepper
½ cup raisins (optional)

Cut the cabbage into chunks that will stand in the feed tube of your food processor and shred, using the slicing disk. Dump it into a big bowl. Cut the ends off the carrots and scrub them well (there's no need to peel them). Shred the carrots, using shredding disk, and add them to the cabbage. Chop the onion with the metal blade, snapping motor off and on, scraping the bowl once or twice.

Scrape the onions into the big bowl and replace the work bowl and steel knife, unwashed. Process the mayonnaise, lemon juice, mustard, sugar, salt, and pepper until combined. Pour over the vegetables; add raisins if desired. Blend thoroughly and chill.

Sweet & Sour Cabbage Soup

The delightfully contrasting flavors of this soup are a creation of my friend Beth.

Serves 8

¼ cup butter
4 carrots, scraped and sliced
3 ribs celery, sliced
2 medium onions, chopped
2 quarts beef stock
Salt and pepper
1 2-pound head green cabbage, chopped
½ cup firmly packed brown sugar
1 cup red wine vinegar

Melt the butter in a large kettle. Sauté the carrots, celery, and onion until tender. Add the stock and season to taste. Simmer, uncovered, for 20 minutes. Stir in the cabbage; simmer 15 minutes more or until cabbage is tender. Add the sugar and vinegar; simmer 10 minutes more. Adjust seasonings. Serve hot, with a crusty loaf of dark bread.

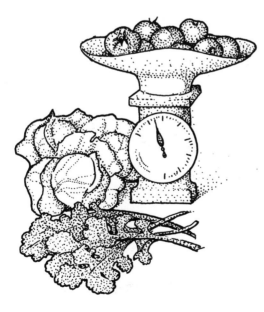

Stuffed Brussels Sprouts

These elegant little finger foods are tasty and different.

Makes 16–20 brussels sprouts

1 pound medium–large brussels sprouts
6 ounces cream cheese, softened
¼ cup finely grated carrots
2 tablespoons finely chopped radishes
2 tablespoons minced green onions
1 tablespoon chopped parsley
1 clove garlic, minced
2 teaspoons chopped fresh thyme (or ½ teaspoon dried)
Salt and pepper
3–4 tablespoons snipped chives

Trim the bases off the sprouts so they will sit solidly. Using the small end of a melon baller or a paring knife, hollow out the cores. Steam the shells over hot water or in the microwave until almost tender and still bright green. Drain, pat dry, and chill.

Combine the cream cheese, carrots, radishes, onions, parsley, garlic, thyme, salt, and pepper. Mix well and spoon into a pastry bag; pipe into the hollows of the sprouts (or use a teaspoon). Sprinkle with chives; chill. Serve cold.

Brussels Sprouts Leaves with Walnut Vinaigrette

Rich and flavorful, this salad is simple to prepare.

Serves 4–5

1 pound brussels sprouts (about 24 medium)
¼ cup chopped red onion
½ cup walnut pieces, toasted
3 tablespoons olive oil
2 tablespoons walnut oil
2 tablespoons white wine vinegar
2 teaspoons fresh lemon juice
2 cloves garlic, minced
1 teaspoon Dijon mustard
Salt and pepper

Trim off the bases of the sprouts. Peel away the outer leaves, snapping them off the base one at a time, until they no longer come off easily. Discard the cores, or save them for soup. You should have about 4 cups of leaves. Put them into a serving bowl with the onion and walnuts. Chill.

In a small jar, combine the oils, vinegar, lemon juice, garlic, mustard, salt, and pepper. Cover and shake well. Drizzle over the mixture in the bowl and toss lightly. Serve right away.

CHAPTER 4

THE FRUIT BASKET

Several weeks into the summer, Midwestern farmers begin to bring large amounts of fruits to the market. It's kind of like dessert, only it comes halfway through the feast.

Truly Mother Nature's candy, the fruits of summer are succulent, sweet and—for a while anyway—abundant. I personally think that the best way to deal with this dazzling profusion is to follow an all-fruit diet. Take various morsels of maximally ripe fruit for breakfast, lunch, and dinner until you've had nothing else for maybe 25 or 30 meals straight and can't stand another bite. Then maybe, just maybe, you'll have had enough.

Till next week, anyhow.

Melons of Many Colors

Midway through the harvest season, the farmer begins to produce an assortment of different-size orbs, each with a hard shell and tasty, nutritious innards. These durable, tasty spheres bring the market some of the sweetest meat the soil has to offer. The melons are here.

Self-contained and lusciously satisfying, a honeydew, Crenshaw melon, or cantaloupe can be a romantic dessert, perhaps filled with plump and flawless fresh berries, at a picnic for two. It even comes all packed and ready to go to a picnic when you buy it.

Of course, larger picnics call for the more generously proportioned Casaba, or the outdoorsy watermelon. (With the watermelon, you also get the bonus of seeds; spitting contests amount to an instant party game.)

But it's more than mere portability which distinguishes the melons. They all provide liberal amounts of vitamin C, and cantaloupe adds generous doses of vitamins A and B—with only about 100 calories in a whole melon. Such a deal!

Long loved for rolling into little spheres and adding to fruit salads, melons are a versatile and economical jewel of summer. In addition to the nutritional windfall they offer, their flavors are delicate and subtle, equally delectable in mixtures and served solo. Quite possibly summer's simplest and finest dessert is a wedge of cantaloupe cradling a scoop of rich vanilla ice cream in its hollow.

And the rinds of melons are useful as well. Cantaloupes and honeydews can be halved and hollowed out and the rinds used as individual bowls, perfect for a fruit compote or a chilled fruit soup (a sprig of mint or a shaving of lemon peel on top might add a natty touch). For a larger serving vessel, nothing beats a decoratively carved watermelon shell.

At the market, look for mature cantaloupes, identified by their corky, gray net-like covering, yellowish skin, and sweet smell. The age-old ripeness test of pressing lightly on the steam end of a cantaloupe may or may not be reliable. Repeated pressing on the end of even an unripe melon will soften it sooner or later. Do check the stem end, though, looking for a calloused, sunken scar. This will tell you that the fruit ripened on the vine, easily pulling loose from its stem at harvest time.

Cantaloupes, and casaba melons too, show their ripeness by softening a bit at the blossom end, opposite the scar. In either fruit, avoid greenish, very firm ones. A ripe casaba is decidely yellow and may have seeds rattling about inside it.

If the cantaloupes aren't yet fully ripe when you bring them home, leave them on the kitchen counter for a day or two. A final ripeness check can be made by poking a seam of the cantaloupe with your fingernail. If the melon crunches, leave it out for another day or so. If the seam yields easily, gobble down a wedge of the melon on the spot, then refrigerate what's left.

Honeydews should be light yellow and slightly tender to thumb pressure. Dark spots on just the surface of the rind are probably harmless, but deeper spots can mean decayed fruit. Greenish-white rinds suggest immaturity.

As for watermelons, there is the best-known variety—those huge, football-shaped monsters rumored sometimes to grow to three tons. But today, particularly at a farmers market, there also are all sorts of other watermelons to be found. Small, spherical watermelons, even sweeter than the big ones, appear at the market, as well as yellow-skinned and seedless varieties.

In any strain, look for firm, symmetrical, unblemished fruit with a dark, crisp stem and a yellowish underside. A firm thump on the rind should bring a dull thud—if you hear a ringing tone, hang up and try again. The melon is immature. Stay away also from springy-feeling watermelons and those with scars resembling healed punctures, which show that worms have been to visit. Don't worry about dark, watery surface spots, as long as they don't seem to have penetrated the flesh.

When a cantaloupe grows too soft or a watermelon just too juicy, they can be pureed into drinks or soup. But try not to let them overripen. Melons really need to be consumed at peak ripeness—when their sugars are fully developed and have not yet begun to break down. Try them too early, and they're relatively hard and flavorless, too late and they're watery—and flavorless.

Watermelon Splash

This is a good use for those scraps you have left over after making lots of melon balls. It's sweet, refreshing, and wholesome.

Serves 6–8

4 cups chunked watermelon
¼ cup fresh lemon juice
Seltzer water
Lime wedges

Put the watermelon and any juice accompanying it into a blender, along with the lemon juice. Liquify the mixture; chill thoroughly.

To serve, pour over ice in a tall glass, filling it ¾ of the way. Top off with seltzer; stir. Add a squeeze of lime and serve.

Cantaloupe Preserves

This unusual spread is delicious and beautifully colored. It uses honey instead of the heaps of sugar sometimes added to preserves.

Makes about 6 half-pints

1 2-pound ripe cantaloupe
2 cups mild honey
2 tablespoons lemon juice

Peel cantaloupe and halve it; scoop out the seeds. Cut it into thin 1-inch slices. In a large glass or ceramic bowl, mix the sliced melon with the honey and lemon juice. Cover and refrigerate overnight.

Place the steeped fruit mixture into a large, nonaluminum kettle and set over high heat. Bring to a boil and cook, stirring constantly, to 9 degrees above the boiling point of water. Boil hard at this temperature, stirring, for one minute.

Take the kettle off the stove. Stir and skim the surface for at least 5 minutes, to prevent floating fruit. Ladle the hot fruit mixture into hot, sterilized jars. Wipe the rims clean and seal. Process for 10 minutes in a boiling-water bath.

Overnight Fruit Compote

Rich and festive, this mixture is good with a special brunch. Of course, the fruit can be cut with a small knife if you have no melon baller.

Serves 8

1 6-ounce can lemonade concentrate, thawed
3 tablespoons orange marmalade
2 tablespoons Cointreau, Grand Marnier, or Triple Sec
4 small, ripe cantaloupes
1 small honeydew melon
1 cup blueberries
1 pint hulled, halved strawberries
2 navel oranges, peeled and sectioned, each section halved
1½ cups diced pineapple (fresh or canned in its own juice),
    optional
8 whole strawberries (for garnish)

Combine the lemonade, marmalade, and liqueur in a small bowl.

Cut the cantaloupes in half. Carefully cut away the pulp from the shell, leaving a wall about ½ inch thick in the shells. Stack and wrap the shells in plastic; chill.

Using a melon baller, roll cantaloupe meat and honeydew into balls. Place them in a large bowl. Add the blueberries, halved strawberries, oranges, and pineapple. Pour the lemonade sauce over the fruit and mix gently. Cover and refrigerate overnight.

At serving time, scoop the fruit into the melon shells, using a slotted spoon. Garnish each serving with a whole strawberry.

Kathi's Melon Ice

Both simple and elegant, this dessert makes the most of the fruit harvest. My friend Kathi likes to serve it with fresh peaches, though it's also wonderful with ripe berries.

Serves 8

4 cups pureed cantaloupe or honeydew melon
¼ cup sugar
1 tablespoon lemon juice (with cantaloupe) or lime juice (with honeydew)
Fresh fruit

Mix everything together in a food processor, then pour into ice-cube trays and freeze until solid. At serving time, dump the frozen cubes back into the food processor and puree again until slushy. Spoon into dessert dishes and top with fresh fruit.

Cantaloupe Soup

Almost a gazpacho, this strictly summertime soup is alive with flavor.

Serves 6

1 large (3-pound) ripe cantaloupe
2 medium–large cucumbers
1 cup plain yogurt
Juice of one lemon
¼ cup chopped basil
2 tablespoons snipped chives
1 large, ripe tomato

Peel the cantaloupe and cucumbers, scoop out their seeds, and place them in a food processor or blender. Puree until smooth. Add the yogurt, lemon juice, basil, and chives. Mix well. Peel the tomato and remove seeds. Chop finely and stir into the soup. Put it into a large bowl and chill for several hours before serving.

Soft Fruits

It someone asked me to name one taste, one single flavor that epitomizes the divine freshness of the summer season, I would have to say the first bite of a really ripe peach.

Rich in vitamins A, B, and C, the peach and its cousins, the plum and the nectarine, sum up with their perfect simplicity the sweet, succinct sensuality of summer. Sure they're delicious in salads, mixed with yogurt, baked in pies, even whirled into blender drinks. But you really can't do better than just eating them out of hand.

Ripe peaches and nectarines are fairly easy to identify. They should be firm, but beginning to soften. The ground color should be white or yellow; if it is green, the fruit was picked too early and won't ripen any further. Round, soft spots suggest bruising or decay and also should be avoided.

In plums, seek out richly colored, barely softening specimens. Immaturity is shown by hardness, poor color quality, and shriveling skin. Also avoid fruit with dull, brown splotches on the skin. The brown tells you that the fruit likely was sunburned and will have poor flavor.

It is important to note that, with any of the soft fruits, you should buy at full ripeness only if you plan to eat them all within the following day or so. Slightly firm fruit can be left in a bowl on the counter—an instant still life!—until it ripens further and grows soft enough to eat. Then store the fruit in the refrigerator until eating time.

Nectarine-Plum Jam

Makes about 8 half-pints

1½ pounds ripe nectarines (about 4–6 medium)
1½ pounds ripe plums (about 8–10)
2 tablespoons lemon juice
1 1⅓-ounce package powdered pectin
3 pounds (7 cups) sugar

Peel nectarines; remove pits. Pit plums (you may leave their skins on). Chop the fruit coarsely and put it into a large, nonaluminum saucepan or a small kettle. Add the lemon juice and pectin. Heat to boiling and cook, stirring, until the mixture reaches a full rolling boil which cannot be stirred down. Add the sugar gradually, stirring all the while. Return the mixture to a rolling boil and boil hard, stirring, for one minute longer.

Remove the kettle from the stove. Stir and skim the foam from the surface before ladling the mixture into hot, sterilized jars (leave ¼-inch headspace). Seal and process in a boiling-water bath for 15 minutes.

Doris's Fresh Peach Daiquiris

Doris Dongvillo and her husband, Adolph, own a fruit farm in St. Joseph, Michigan.

Makes 4 daiquiris

1 6-ounce can lemonade or limeade
1 can water
1 can light rum
1 cup sliced peaches
6–7 ice cubes

Whirl all the ingredients together in a blender until smooth. Serve immediately or freeze until ready to serve (the alcohol in the rum will keep the drinks from freezing).

Mother Nature's Bonbons

In a season fraught with freshness, like the farmer's harvest season, it's hard to imagine what more one could possibly want from the yield. Farmer and consumer perhaps even grow complacent, taking for granted the ready supply of fresh-picked goodness. And then something comes along that's really worth celebrating: the berries! Once again we are reminded how special—and how fleeting—this time of year is.

The farmer presents these cherished crops with extraordinary pride. "We've been picking raspberries for three weeks already," he'll say, cautioning, "Next week might be the last of them." A trace of wistfulness lingering on his face, he'll gingerly wrap your raspberries and send you on home to enjoy them.

The various berries appear more or less in succession, spanning the entire market season. It's a wonderful aspect of the cosmic design that we are at no point left completely without them. But none of them is available at the market anywhere near long enough. So enjoy them. Stuff yourself with them. Throw a tray full of them into the freezer. If the weather is cool, put up a batch of jam or a tangy conserve. Or try a special dessert.

The berries tend to be fragile and need some special care. Hustle them home from the market and put them, unwashed, into the refrigerator, preferably spread in a single layer. Discard any moldy berries without hesitating, because mold is highly contagious if you happen to be a berry.

Strawberries tend to turn up at the market earliest. Little ruby jewels, these heart-shaped fruits are packed with vitamin C and fiber. They are at their best when they look clean and bright red in color, ideally with small, sparsely numbered seeds. One rather reliable test is a quick whiff: ripe strawberries have a heady, sweet, and inviting aroma.

Blueberries indulge us with a relatively long harvest. If you try hard, you can almost get enough of them. At their ripest, they will be a deep, dark blue and quite pleasingly plump. For cooking purposes, it helps to buy ones that are fairly uniform in size. Avoid any baskets with more than a couple of shriveled blueberries in them—they are probably old. Moisture also is bad news, indicating a breakdown of the fruit. Blueberries that have been allowed to overripen will look dull and lifeless.

These two venerable berries—the strawberry and the blue-berry—are true treats, but as far as I'm concerned, the raspberry is the crown jewel of summer's berry blitz. Deep red, vaguely opalescent, and delicately plump, the perfect raspberry is quite possibly the best "as is" dessert the fruit farmer can offer. A crystal goblet brimming with ripe red raspberries is an insufferably elegant indulgence.

Raspberries and their cousins the blackberries, dewberries, and loganberries appear so briefly as to leave us hollering for more. Although some farmers have late-season berries, suitable for picking well into the fall, summer's first tease of the sublime raspberry is the sweetest, and it's invariably too short.

As flavorful as they are fragile, these members of the Rubus botanical clan will show peak ripeness by being clean and dry with solid, vivid color. Unripe fruit is evidenced by caps that remained adhered to the fruit at harvest time. Too-ripe raspberries are soft, leaky, and dull in color. Check the container—if it shows a lot of staining, these ephemeral berries already have had their day.

Sweet cherries, though not berries, seem to go along with the bite-size crowd and are another of summer's most eloquent statements. Sweeter than honey, a black-red cherry makes a satisfying, refreshing summer snack.

Ripe cherries have firm, dark, shiny skin. Dry stems and brown discoloration signal decayed fruit.

However you choose to enjoy the little fruits, remember to buy enough—a small carton of ripe berries bought by a hungry shopper has scarcely a chance of making it home from the market. If you want to buy a lot, try going to the market about 20 minutes before it is scheduled to close. The farmer might be happy to haggle a little with a high-volume customer like you, and he just possibly could offer you a can't-beat-it deal. He probably would welcome the opportunity not to have to cart it all home with him.

But really, these miniature sweet meats usually deserve their high price. Such are the laws of supply and demand. While they're around, these enigmatic yummies are definitely in demand.

Anyway, you're worth it.

Fresh Strawberry-Bran Tart

Serves 6

1 10-inch bran pie crust, baked (recipe follows)
1 quart fresh strawberries
⅓ cup turbinado ("raw") sugar
1 tablespoon cornstarch
Pinch of salt
Whipped cream

Wash and sort the berries. Hull and halve the best-looking ones to make about 2 cups of prepared fruit. Spread them, cut side down, across the baked crust.

Hull the remaining berries and puree them. Place in a medium saucepan and bring to the boiling point. Mix in the sugar, cornstarch, and salt. Cook stirring, for 3 minutes. Push through a sieve and spread over the berries in the shell. Chill thoroughly. At serving time, smother the pie with whipped cream.

Bran Pie Crust

Here is a good foundation for any fruit pie. Or you might like it with some sort of creamy filling—yogurt, perhaps.

1½ cups lightly crushed bran flakes (about 3 cups whole flakes)
¼ cup flour
¼ teaspoon nutmeg
2 tablespoons butter, melted
½ cup apple juice or cider

Preheat oven to 425°F.

Blend the crushed flakes, flour, and nutmeg. Stir in the butter and cider; blend well. Press evenly into a 10-inch tart pan, extending the top slightly above the rim of the pan. Bake at 425°F for 10–12 minutes. Cool completely before filling.

Strawberry Soufflé

Cool and elegant, this dish can be made using berries that are just a little too ripe to serve plain. Save a few perfect ones, if you have them, for garnishing.

Serves 4

1½ cups fresh strawberries
⅓ cup honey
½ cup water
1 tablespoon fresh lemon juice
¼ teaspoon ground cinnamon
1 envelope unflavored gelatin
2 egg whites, at room temperature
⅛ teaspoon salt
½ cup heavy cream, whipped
3 or 4 whole strawberries (optional)

Fit a 3-cup soufflé dish with a 2-inch foil collar; secure with string.

Wash and hull the berries and puree them in a food mill, blender, or food processor. You should have about a cup of puree.

Mix the honey, water, lemon juice, and cinnamon in a small saucepan. Sprinkle the gelatin over the liquid, and stir over low heat about 3 minutes to dissolve the gelatin. Remove from heat; stir in the pureed berries. Blend thoroughly. Chill, stirring occasionally, until the mixture mounds slightly when dropped from a spoon.

Beat the egg whites in a large bowl until stiff but not dry. Fold in the gelatin mixture, then the whipped cream.

Turn into the prepared dish; chill for at least 4 hours. Garnish with berries, if desired, and serve cold.

Strawberry Margaritas

Fix these when it's hot out and you've had a long day.

Serves 2

12–14 medium-size ripe strawberries
3 ounces tequila
1½ ounce Cointreau or Triple Sec
⅓ cup pineapple juice
1 ounce Rose's lime juice
8–10 ice cubes
Lime wedges
Sugar

Place the berries, tequila, Cointreau, juices, and ice in a blender; puree until smooth. Rub the rim of each glass with a piece of lime to moisten it. Pour a layer of sugar into a saucer or other small plate and invert the glasses into the sugar, coating the rims. Carefully pour in the drink mixture, hang a slice of lime on the rim, and think of a good toast.

Nana's Strawberry Jam

Included in my mom's recipe file is this one, in my great-grand-mother Nana's handwriting. It reads like this:

Equal parts strawberries and sugar. Leave berries whole. Let stand in sugar several hours before cooking. Put on fire and when boiling BRISKLY, cook exactly 5 minutes. Take off fire and let cool thoroughly, then repeat boiling process. Pour into glasses. Put on paraffin after jam is cold.

The yield for this jam varies according to how many berries you have. If you use 3 pounds (about 7 cups) of sugar and 2 quarts (about 3 pounds) of berries, expect about 4 half-pints.

Blueberry Oatmeal Muffins

These are tasty and not too sweet. Be careful to add the berries gently, or you will end up with blue batter.

Makes 10–12 muffins

1 cup rolled oats
1 cup plain yogurt
1 cup unbleached white flour
¼ cup sugar
1 tablespoon baking powder
¼ teaspoon salt
¼ teaspoon nutmeg
⅛ teaspoon cinnamon
1 egg, beaten
2 tablespoons water
¼ cup vegetable oil
¾ cup fresh blueberries

Preheat the oven to 400°F. Lightly grease a 12-cup muffin pan.

Combine the oats and yogurt; let stand 10 minutes. Meanwhile, sift together the flour, sugar, baking powder, salt, nutmeg, and cinnamon. Make a well in the center of the dry ingredients. Beat the egg with the water in a medium bowl; mix in the oat-yogurt mixture and oil. Stir into the well in the dry ingredients, mixing just until everything is moistened. Fold in blueberries. Fill greased muffin cups ¾ of the way. Bake muffins for 20 minutes at 400°F until lightly browned.

Blueberry Brancakes

Top these nutritious and yummy pancakes with yogurt and honey or warm maple syrup.

Serves 5–6

1 cup flour
¼ cup sugar
2½ teaspoons baking powder
½ teaspoon salt
¼ teaspoon nutmeg
1 cup milk
1 egg, lightly beaten
¼ cup vegetable oil
¾ cup miller's (unprocessed) bran
1 cup fresh blueberries

Mix the flour, sugar, baking powder, salt, and nutmeg together in a large bowl.

In a small bowl, beat the milk, egg, and oil; stir into the dry ingredients, mixing just until blended. Fold in the bran and berries.

Ladle out onto a hot, lightly greased griddle and cook over medium–low heat until nicely browned, turning once.

Blueberry Buckle

This old-fashioned dessert is a summertime favorite. Try it warm from the oven.

Serves 8

2 cups sifted flour
2 teaspoons baking powder
½ teaspoon salt
¼ cup butter
¾ cup sugar
1 egg
½ cup milk
2 cups blueberries
Topping (recipe follows)

Preheat the oven to 375°F.

In a medium bowl, sift together the flour, baking powder, and salt. Set aside.

Cream the butter and sugar in a large bowl; beat in the egg. Add the flour mixture and the milk, stirring only until everything is moistened. Fold in the blueberries gently.

Turn into a greased 8- or 9-inch square cake pan. Spread with topping.

Bake at 375°F for 45 minutes. Loosen the edges on removal from the oven; let cool in the pan.

Topping

½ cup sugar
⅓ cup flour
½ teaspoon cinnamon
½ cup soft butter

Mix well.

Blueberry Shrub

Thirst-quenching and quite delicious.

1 pint blueberries
¼ cup sugar
1 cup orange juice
⅓ cup fresh lemon juice
Seltzer
Orange slices

Puree the berries in a food mill, blender, or food processor. Using a stainless steel or enameled saucepan, mix the berry puree and the sugar and bring to a simmer, stirring constantly. Stir in the orange and lemon juices and chill thoroughly. Serve over crushed ice, adding seltzer to taste. Garnish with an orange slice, if desired.

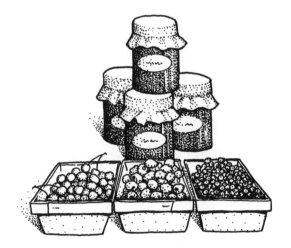

Raspberry-Rhubarb Muffins

These seasonal muffins are equally good at breakfast or tea.

Makes a dozen muffins

1 cup rolled oats
1 cup buttermilk
1 cup unbleached white flour
½ cup sugar
2 teaspoons baking powder
1 teaspoon baking soda
¼ teaspoon salt
¼ teaspoon nutmeg
Pinch of cinnamon
1 egg, beaten
¼ cup oil
1 cup finely diced rhubarb
1½ cups fresh raspberries

Preheat the oven to 400°F. Grease a 12-cup muffin pan and line cups with muffin papers.

Mix the oats and buttermilk. Let stand for 10 minutes.

In a large bowl, combine the flour, sugar, baking powder, soda, salt, nutmeg, and cinnamon. Make a well in the center.

Beat together the egg and oil; add the oats. Mix gently into the flour mixture, stirring just to blend. Mix in the rhubarb, then the raspberries, very gently. Spoon into paper-lined muffin pan, filling cups ¾ of the way up. Bake at 400°F for 20–25 minutes, until golden brown. Cool 10 minutes in the pan, then remove to a wire rack to finish cooling.

Fresh Raspberry Soup

Unusual and quick to prepare, this soup is perfect for a hot day when you just don't feel much like cooking.

Serves 6

4 cups orange juice
2 cups plain yogurt
1 cup sour cream
1 cup buttermilk
1½ tablespoons honey
2 tablespoons fresh lemon juice
¼ teaspoon nutmeg
Pinch of cinnamon
3 cups fresh raspberries
Thin orange slices

Place everything except the berries and orange slices in a large bowl and whisk or beat with a hand mixer until very smooth.

Wash the berries and divide between serving bowls. Ladle the soup over them and garnish each bowl with an orange slice.

Raspberry Bread

A slice of this moist loaf tastes especially good with a bit of cream cheese spread on top.

Makes 2 loaves

2 cups fresh raspberries
3¼ cups unbleached white flour
2 cups firmly packed brown sugar
1½ teaspoons cinnamon
1 teaspoon nutmeg
1¼ teaspoons baking soda
1 teaspoon salt
1¼ cups vegetable oil
4 eggs, beaten
1 cup chopped walnuts

Preheat the oven to 350°F. Grease and flour two 9″ × 5″ loaf pans.

Place the raspberries in a large bowl and lightly crush them with your fingertips. They should have a chunky-mush consistency to them.

Mix the flour, sugar, cinnamon, nutmeg, soda, and salt in a large bowl, using your fingers to blend everything well.

Blend the oil and eggs into the berries and add to the flour mixture, stirring just to blend. Fold in the walnuts.

Divide the batter evenly between the two prepared pans. Bake for 45–50 minutes at 350°F, until a toothpick inserted in the center comes out clean.

Cool the loaves for 10 minutes in the pans, then turn them out onto a wire rack to finish cooling.

Fresh Raspberry Pudding

This dessert is moist and sweet. It's a good way to use raspberries that are a little too juicy.

Serves 6

1 pint fresh red raspberries
Juice of ½ lemon
3 tablespoons butter, softened
1¾ cups sugar, divided
1 cup unbleached white flour
1 teaspoon baking powder
½ teaspoon salt, divided
¼ teaspoon nutmeg
½ cup milk
1 tablespoon cornstarch
1 cup boiling water

Preheat the oven to 350°F.

Grease and flour an 8-inch square pan. Spread the berries in the pan; sprinkle the lemon juice evenly over them.

Beat the butter and ¾ cup of the sugar in a large bowl. Mix the flour, baking powder, ¼ teaspoon of the salt, and the nutmeg. Add to the sugar mixture alternately with the milk. Spread over the berries.

Combine the remaining cup of sugar, the cornstarch, and the remaining ¼ teaspoon of salt. Sprinkle over the cake batter. Carefully pour the boiling water evenly over everything. Bake for an hour at 350°F. Serve warm or at room temperature, topped with vanilla ice cream.

Cherry Cordial Bread Pudding

This is a wanton exercise in gluttony. Go for it.

Serves 8–10

1 pint sweet cherries, halved and pitted
¼ cup Amaretto
3 ounces unsweetened chocolate
1 cup whipping cream
3 cups milk
3 eggs
1 cup sugar
¼ teaspoon nutmeg
1 loaf day-old French bread, torn into bite-size pieces
   (about 7 cups)
2 tablespoons butter, melted

Toss the cherries with the Amaretto in a medium bowl. Cover and let stand about an hour, stirring now and then.

Preheat the oven to 325°F. Generously butter a 3-quart baking dish.

Melt the chocolate in the top of a double boiler; set aside to cool.

In a large bowl, mix the cream, milk, eggs, sugar, and nutmeg. Stir in the cooled chocolate; blend thoroughly. Add the bread and the cherry mixture. Stir well, then mix in the butter.

Turn into the prepared baking dish and bake until golden and crusty, about an hour. Cool on a wire rack. Serve warm, topped with ice cream.

CHAPTER 5

HIGH SEASON
THE TIDAL WAVE

A trip to the farmers market at the height of the harvest season is a comforting excursion into the land of plenty. The farmer is inundated with ripe everything. His tables creak under the weight of the soil's largess. Now all you have to do is find some way to make the most of it all.

At no other time of year is the consumer faced with a more delicious dilemma. Here are all these fabulous vegetables, all reaching their absolute peak, apparently on the same day. What do you reach for first? A handful of beans and a few summer squashes? A couple ears of corn and an eggplant? How about a basket of tomatoes, some pea pods, and half a dozen multi-hued peppers? It's all so overwhelming.

So try everything, though not necessarily all today. Truthfully, you can spread it out over another week or two. This peak-season flood will be on for at least that long. But hurry. One taste certainly will not be enough.

Beans

The heartland harvest of the family *Phaseolus* amounts to more—much more—than a hill of beans. A mountain might be more like it.

By mid-summer, the farmer is appearing at the weekly market with enormous crates of beans in tow. First come the tender, sweet snap beans, lusciously tempting out of hand and even better quickly steamed and kissed with a light coat of butter. Later come the tasty and adaptable shell beans, which are simply the mature bean seeds, ripened in the pod.

All of the beans come in huge quantities. Do keep your head; you can only eat so many and still enjoy the perfect ripeness they bring with them to the market.

Little nuggets of nutritional power, beans are one of the healthiest items grown on the farm. Snap beans are rich in vitamin A and calcium, and the shell varieties offer B vitamins, high-quality carbohydrates and incomplete proteins.

In snap beans, try to find skinny ones, or at least a batch all of the same general size. The tenderest ones will have tiny seeds. The beans should look fresh and unblemished, brightly colored (whether yellow or green), and should snap easily. Steer clear of limp, flabby pods and those that are very thick, which probably means overmaturity.

The shell beans—limas, favas, and horticulturals—are at their best when the pods are filled out, clean, and a bit shiny. If the beans are too old the pods will be hard and discolored, perhaps streaked with brown.

French Green Bean Salad

My grandmother used to do this with leftover beans.

Serves 4

2 cups thinly French-cut green beans, cooked until barely tender
¼ cup mayonnaise
2 tablespoons minced onion (yellow, red, or green)
1 tablespoon chopped fresh dill weed

Mix everything and chill. Serve on a bed of nice-looking lettuce.

Sweet & Sour Green Beans

Piquant and a "snap" to put together.

Serves 6–8

1½ pounds fresh snap beans
½ cup dark brown sugar
1 10½-ounce can condensed tomato soup
½ pound bacon, cooked crisp and crumbled

Preheat the oven to 350°F.
   Wash, trim, and slice the beans. You should have about 6 cups. Steam them in a small amount of water until just barely crisp-tender. Combine with the remaining ingredients and bake in a buttered casserole for 1 hour at 350°F.

Two-Day Vegetable Beef Soup

You might want to stick a few green beans into the freezer and save them for a good wintry day, to make the most of this soul-warming Crockpot soup.

Serves 6

1 medium onion, chopped
¾ pound snap beans, cut into 1-inch lengths
1 cup chopped celery
1 cup sliced, scraped carrots
1 cup diced, peeled potatoes
1 16-ounce can tomatoes
2 tablespoons chopped parsley
1 teaspoon salt
1½ teaspoons Worcestershire sauce
Pepper to taste
2 pounds cross-cut beef shanks (4–5 pieces)

Put everything into a Crockpot, putting the meat on top. Add water to cover ingredients (2–3 cups) and stir. Cover and cook on low for at least 12 hours; more (up to 36 hours) is better. Add more water as necessary. Turn up to high for the last 5–7 hours. Before serving, remove the bones and shred the meat into bite-size pieces. Stir back into the pot and ladle out hot soup. You might want a good crusty loaf of bread to dunk into this hearty bowl full of supper.

Lima Beans With Sour Cream

My mom says, "People who hate lima beans beg for this recipe."
It's rich and luscious.

Serves 8

3 pounds fresh lima beans (in pods)
1 clove garlic, cut in half
1½ cups sour cream
⅓ cup butter, melted
1 tablespoon dry mustard
1 tablespoon molasses
Salt to taste

Preheat the oven to 350°F.

Shell the beans and steam over boiling water until barely tender, about 15 minutes.

Rub a 2-quart casserole with the garlic. Mix the remaining ingredients in a large bowl; stir in the beans. Turn into the casserole and bake for an hour at 350°F.

Corn

If there were no such thing as corn, I'm quite convinced that spring would dribble right into autumn, and there would be no summer at all. No other vegetable sums up the ease of the summer attitude quite as articulately as corn.

Not technically a vegetable, corn is a whole grain which comes as close to table-ready as any grain we know. Just a few minutes in a kettle of boiling water is all that stands between you and an earful of sheer nirvana.

Freshness is of paramount importance when you prepare corn. The instant the cobs are cut from the stalk, their sugars begin to break down into starch. After only a few hours, the corn tastes a good deal less sweet than it did right after picking.

At the market, choose ears wrapped snugly in bright green husks. The silk ends should be dried and free of decay and worm injury. If you peel back the husk and pierce a kernel with your fingernail, a milky liquid should squirt out (if the corn is one of the super-sweet varieties, the fluid will be clear).

You can confirm the corn's freshness by checking the stem end. If it was picked within the previous half-day or so, the cut surface will be pale green and moist. If it's been just one day since it stood in the field, the stem scar will look whitish. And if the ears are more than a day old, the site of the cut will have turned brownish.

While corn is arguably best after a quick meeting with a pot of boiling water, it also plays a delectable lead to a considerable variety of supporting casts. It can be baked into a casserole, napped with a little cream (sweet or sour) and sprinkled with crumbled bacon, or folded into almost any concoction of leftovers. Add a handful of kernels to a crock of chili, tuck some into an omelette, or fold a few into your favorite cornbread batter. Throw a cup or two into just about any batch of soup, or mix some into your next quiche. And if you add corn to a legume-based dish, like seasoned pintos, black-eyed peas, or Boston baked beans, you'll create a nourishing, filling source of complete protein—to say nothing of the delicious meal you'll enjoy.

Barbecue-Glazed Corn

Stick a few ears of this foil-wrapped corn on the grate alongside your meat the next time you fire up the barbecue grill.

For each ear, allow:

2 teaspoons butter
1 teaspoon minced onion
½ teaspoon brown sugar
Salt and pepper to taste

Melt the butter in a small saucepan. Sauté the onion in it just until tender. Add the sugar and stir until it is dissolved.

Shuck the ears of corn, removing as much silk as you comfortably can. Place each cob diagonally on a generous square of heavy-duty foil. Brush liberally with the butter mixture; sprinkle with salt and pepper.

Wrap the foil around the corn, sealing tight. Place on the grill and cook for 25–35 minutes or until done, turning often.

Corn Pudding

This simple, homey dish offers creamy richness and lots of protein.
Serves 6

4 cups corn kernels, uncooked
½ cup butter
1 tablespoon salt
2 teaspoons sugar
6 eggs, lightly beaten

Preheat the oven to 350°F. Butter a 2-quart casserole or soufflé dish.

Combine the corn, butter, salt, and sugar in a medium saucepan. Heat until hot to the touch. Stir in the beaten eggs. Turn into the prepared dish. Set it into a larger pan, filled with hot water to a depth of about 2 inches. Bake at 350°F for about 50 minutes, until puffed and golden. Serve hot.

Scalloped Corn

A hearty side dish, this mixture involves more work than just dunking the ears into boiling water, but the raves you'll receive will make the effort worthwhile.

Serves 3–4

4 tablespoons butter, divided
½ medium onion, chopped
½ green pepper, diced
2 tablespoons flour
1 teaspoon salt
½ teaspoon dry mustard
¼ teaspoon paprika
Pinch of cayenne
½ cup milk
1½ cups corn kernels
1 egg yolk, lightly beaten
2 slices day-old white bread, torn into small pieces
⅔ cup crushed Ritz or Town House crackers

Melt 2 tablespoons of the butter in a medium saucepan. Sauté the onion and green pepper until softened, then stir in the flour, salt, mustard, paprika, and cayenne. Cook, stirring, for a minute or two. Stir in the milk and cook, stirring, until thickened. Add the corn and egg yolk. Remove from the heat.

Melt another tablespoon of butter in a small skillet. Add the bread pieces and toss until toasted. Stir into the corn mixture. Turn into a buttered casserole.

Melt the remaining tablespoon of butter in the same skillet. Add the cracker crumbs, tossing until coated. Spread over the top of the casserole. Bake in a 400°F oven for 10–15 minutes or until crumbs are browned. Serve immediately.

Corn Chowder

This flavorful soup makes a respectable supper entree.

Serves 4

2 potatoes, peeled and diced
2 medium ears fresh sweet corn, scraped
2½ cups chicken stock
Pinch of salt
3 strips thin-sliced bacon, diced
½ green pepper, seeded and chopped
1 onion, chopped
2 ribs celery, chopped
3 tablespoons flour
1½ cups milk
1 bay leaf
2–3 tablespoons chopped parsley
Salt and pepper to taste
Pinch of nutmeg
½ cup plain yogurt

Cook the diced potatoes in lightly salted stock for 4–5 minutes. Add the corn and boil until the vegetables are tender, another 6–8 minutes or so. Strain off the cooking liquid and reserve for the chowder.

Cook the bacon until crisp, using a large saucepan or small kettle. Remove from the pan with a slotted spoon and set aside. Drain off all but 3 tablespoons of the bacon fat. Cook the green pepper, onion, and celery in the reserved fat until lightly colored, about 6–7 minutes. Sprinkle on the flour and blend well. Stir in the reserved potato liquid, milk, bay leaf, parsley, salt, pepper, and nutmeg. Bring to a boil and cook for 2–3 minutes. Stir in the potatoes and corn; remove from the heat and let mellow at room temperature for 30–45 minutes.

Remove the bay leaf. Reheat the chowder gently, adjusting seasoning as desired. Stir in the yogurt and reserved bacon at the last minute; heat briefly and serve.

Cucumbers

As the season progresses, lots of clues signal the genuine arrival of summer: the end of the school year, the opening of the local pool, the blooming of the peonies. For me, though, summer *really* comes in with cucumbers. When the farmer puts a mound of the sweet green cylinders out on his market table, I know the summer has finally, irrevocably begun.

Once ripened, this crisp, refreshing vegetable is fairly fragile. Composed largely of water, a cucumber begins to shrivel up soon after it is picked. So try to keep your purchasing zeal in check, buying only as many as you will eat in the next few days.

Choose firm, crisp cucumbers with good green color. The excessively large, yellow, wrinkly or puffy ones are old and tough and will taste bitter. They'll also have seeds of a size that introduces the hazard of choking.

Once home, wash the cucumbers and store them in the vegetable hydrator section of the refrigerator—or in a more humid spot, if you've got one. They love that moisture.

Cucumbers also are finicky about temperatures: if kept too warm they'll continue ripening. Too cold, and they'll turn mushy.

There is plenty of individual leeway allowed in preparing cucumbers. Some people love the skin. For them, leave it on—it adds a bit of fiber. But if the cucumbers have been waxed (a marketing trick to help keep in moisture), the skin will carry a decidedly bitter flavor, and you'll want to peel it off. If the peel tastes OK but looks unexciting, try scoring the cucumber lengthwise with a fork, or peeling it with a paring knife in alternating strips for a sort of striped effect. If, after peeling, you still notice some bitterness, try scoring the peeled cucumber with a fork. This will release some of the sub-flesh juices and mellow the flavor a bit.

Large cucumbers, while often still delicately tasty, may have seeds that are tough and large enough to require removal. Simply halve the cucumber lengthwise and scoop out the seed cavity with a teaspoon. If the cucumber isn't overly mature, there should be enough flesh remaining to let you feel you're not throwing most of the vegetable away.

As for eating, cucumbers are wonderful all alone: thirst-quenching, crunchy, and satisfying—good diet food. My daughter adores them. Sometimes they're the only vegetable she'll permit on her plate.

But their subtle flavor blends so well with such a wide variety of other foods, it's almost a shame to use cucumbers solo. Wonderful with fish, they also team nicely with peppers and onions and are a refreshing addition to fresh vegetable sauces. With all that water in them, they're good for thinning purees and soups. And few uses are more elegant than slicing them thin and placing them between similarly thin slices of bread. Make it cheese bread, lightly toasted, and add a little minced onion, some watercress, and a touch of good mayonnaise, and you've created a memorable luncheon treat.

Cucumber-Yogurt Salad

Fresh basil and yogurt bring new potential to a familiar summer salad mixture.

Serves 8

3 large cucumbers
1 medium red onion
1½ cups plain yogurt
¼ cup wine vinegar
1½ tablespoons fresh lemon juice
3 tablespoons minced fresh basil
1 large clove garlic, minced
1½ teaspoons Dijon mustard
Salt and pepper to taste

Peel the cucumbers and halve lengthwise. Scoop out the seeds. Slice the cucumbers thin and place them in a large bowl. Peel, quarter, and thinly slice the onion. Toss with the cucumbers, cover, and chill.

Mix the remaining ingredients in a covered jar; refrigerate. Toss the two mixtures together at serving time.

Cucumber-Dill Dressing

My friend Beth developed this savory mixture. It's a perfect way to top summer's glorious greens.

Makes about 2½ cups

2 large cucumbers
1 cup mayonnaise
1 cup sour cream
3 tablespoons chopped dill weed
Dash of Tabasco
1 tablespoon wine vinegar
Seasoning salt or Spice Islands Beau Monde seasoning, to taste

Peel and seed the cucumbers. Puree them in a blender or food processor.

Combine the remaining ingredients in a medium bowl and mix thoroughly. Stir in the cucumber puree and blend well. Adjust seasonings if necessary. Chill for at least an hour before using.

Eggplant

Among the farmer's most elegant offerings is an egg-shaped jewel with the color of a dark amethyst and the patina of a fine opal—the smooth and versatile eggplant.

This relative newcomer is a welcome entry at the mid-summer market. For many years eggplant remained a crop exclusive to warm climates. But now that short-season varieties have been established, market shoppers in even the northernmost regions can enjoy the vegetable fresh off the farm.

Slightly more labor-intensive than a lot of other crops, eggplant needs to be sliced, salted, and left in a colander to drain for half an hour or so before it is cooked. After the 30 minutes, just squeeze out the liquid gently and blot the slices dry. This step helps rid the vegetable of some of its excess moisture, ensuring a firmer result. And if you plan to sauté the slices, the draining also will prevent them from absorbing too much oil as they cook.

Eggplant has plenty of redeeming qualities. You can dress it up—breading, sautéeing, and blanketing it with tomato sauce and cheeses is a justifiably popular route. But it also tastes wonderful all alone: grilled outdoors and drizzled with herb butter, sautéed with garlic and seasonings, broiled, baked, or steamed. It is a substantial vegetable, used in many parts of Asia as a main-dish staple.

In the market, go for smallish eggplants that are firm, glossy, and heavy for their size, with taut, deeply colored, and unblemished skin. The surface should yield slightly to the gentle pressure of your fingers, but then spring back when you release it. If the indentations remain, the eggplant is too ripe. The cap should still be on, helping to keep the moisture intact. Stay away from over-sized eggplants, which tend to be seedy and perhaps mushy in texture. Those with wrinkly skin, brown spots, and a flabby feel to them are likely to have some decay or a bitter taste, or both.

Eggplant Roulade with Sauce Aurore

A showstopping, meat-free entree served in a pool of fresh tomato cream sauce.

Serves 6

Soufflé

¼ cup butter
5 tablespoons flour
1½ cups milk, warmed
5 eggs, separated
Salt to taste
A few grains cayenne
½ cup freshly ground Romano cheese

Filling

1 medium eggplant, diced fine, salted, and drained
2 tablespoons olive oil
2 medium shallots, minced
1 medium clove garlic, minced
½ cup fresh bread crumbs
¼ cup chopped parsley
1 tablespoon chopped fresh rosemary
½ teaspoon dried thyme
Salt and pepper to taste
1 cup finely shredded cheddar cheese
Half & half

Sauce

1 large, ripe tomato
2 tablespoons butter
2 tablespoons flour
1 cup half & half
Salt and pepper to taste
Fresh rosemary sprigs (optional garnish)

Preheat the oven to 400°F. Lightly butter a 10″ × 5″ jelly roll pan. Line with wax paper. Butter and lightly flour the paper.

For the soufflé, melt the butter in a medium saucepan. Stir in the flour; cook, stirring, for a minute or two. Stir in the milk and continue cooking and stirring until thickened. Season to taste and remove from the heat.

Beat the egg yolks, then dribble in some of the hot white sauce, stirring briskly. Mix well, then return to the saucepan and blend. Stir in the Romano cheese and set aside.

Beat the egg whites with a little salt until stiff peaks form. Fold a spoonful or two into the sauce to lighten it, then fold in the rest of the whites gently.

Spread the mixture evenly across the prepared pan, getting it into all the corners. Bake at 400°F for about 15 minutes, or until puffy and golden. Cool on a rack, then invert onto a smooth, clean surface. Peel off wax paper.

For the filling, sauté the drained eggplant in olive oil until lightly colored and barely tender; remove with a slotted spoon. Lightly sauté the shallots and garlic in the same pan, adding more oil if needed. Remove from the heat; stir in the crumbs, seasonings, and eggplant. Mix well, then add the cheddar cheese. Blend thoroughly.

Spread the filling evenly over the baked soufflé base. Roll up carefully, starting at one of the short edges. Put on a baking pan; brush lightly with half & half and cover loosely with foil. Bake about 20 minutes at 400°F. Prepare the sauce while the roulade is baking.

For the sauce, spear the tomato on a fork and toast it over the flame of a gas stove until the skin splits (or dunk into a pan of boiling water for 30 seconds). Rinse under cold running water, slipping off the skin. Quarter the tomato and scoop out the seeds. Puree the tomato pulp in a blender or food mill. Set aside.

Melt the butter in a small saucepan until bubbly. Stir in the flour and cook over medium heat, still stirring, for a minute or two. Whisk in the half & half and salt and pepper and stir until thickened. Remove about ¼ cup of the sauce and reserve. Stir the tomato puree into the remaining sauce.

To serve, cut the warm roulade into 12 slices, each about ¾ inch thick. Spoon about 2 tablespoons of the tomato sauce onto each of six plates, spreading it out to cover the bottom. Arrange two roulade slices on top of the sauce. Put the reserved white sauce into a squirt bottle, if you have one, or dip into it with a point-ended teaspoon. Drizzle a little white sauce in a circle around each serving of roulade; swirl slightly with a dull knife. Garnish with rosemary and serve immediately.

Eggplant Salsa

This chunky, savory sauce is superb with roast or grilled lamb. But you might also try tucking it into a pita round, or using it as a pizza topping with a good provolone cheese.

Makes about 3 cups

1 tablespoon olive oil
2 tablespoons butter
1 medium eggplant, cut into ¼-inch cubes, salted and drained
1 cup chopped red onion
2 cloves garlic, minced
1 large tomato, peeled, seeded, and chopped
2 teaspoons chopped fresh dill weed
1 teaspoon chopped fresh rosemary
¼ cup freshly grated Romano or Parmesan cheese

Heat the oil and butter in a large skillet. Sauté the eggplant and onion in it until just tender; stir in the garlic and cook another minute or two. Remove from the heat; toss in the tomato, herbs, and cheese. Let the salsa sit for one hour to allow the flavors to blend. Serve at room temperature.

Peas

Actually, by mid-season the pea crop is almost winding down. Generally an early arrival at the market, sweet peas span most of the first couple of months of the harvest. They are terrific little nuggets of iron and B vitamins, and a good source of complex carbohydrates. And half a cup of them provides more fiber than a bowl of many kinds of bran cereal.

Whether you choose garden peas, which must be shelled, or the less labor-intensive edible-podded sugar peas, prepare for a treat. Usually available just until the assault of summer's most ferocious heat, farm-fresh peas present a fleeting sample of some of the grower's choicest work.

When perfectly ripe, sweet peas have crisp, firm pods of a dazzling bright green color. The pods should snap, not bend, and have sort of a velvety sheen about them. They should be snugly packed full of peas. Pods that are swollen, poorly colored, spotted with gray or wet spots, and those that are limp and wrinkled should be avoided—they've been around too long. Immature pods are dark green or wilted and flat.

Because the pod functions as a protective jacket, never buy peas already shelled—I don't care how low your energy level is. The peas will be tough, flavorless, and the color of an avocado. Yuck.

And don't shell the peas too long before cooking them, either. The exposure to open air speeds up the breakdown of the peas' sugars and hastens the loss of tenderness. In this respect peas are akin to sweet corn. With either crop, you should ideally accompany the farmer to the field, bringing along a kettle of water and a portable stove. That way, you can snatch the pod from the vine and evacuate the peas directly into a quick, scalding bath—all in one smooth movement.

But if that doesn't fit into your schedule, or his, try to be first in line when he sets up his table at the market.

Fresh Pea Soup

If you think pea soup has to be made with dried splits, think again. This zesty, colorful mixture is quickly prepared and full of fresh summer flavors.

Makes about 3 cups

1 12-ounce can V-8 juice
1 teaspoon cornstarch
2 pounds fresh sweet peas, shelled (about 2 cups)
1 large red bell pepper, chopped fine
2 teaspoons chopped basil
1 or 2 scallions sliced (include some of the green part)

Combine the juice and cornstarch in a medium saucepan. Stir in the peas, red pepper, and basil. Bring to a boil over medium heat, stirring constantly. Cover and simmer gently for about 5 minutes, stirring often, until the vegetables are tender. Serve hot, sprinkled with the sliced scallion.

Fresh Pea and Rice Salad

This satisfying salad puts leftover rice to delicious use.

Serves 3–4

½ cup freshly shucked peas (about ½ pound)
¼ cup pine nuts
2 cups cooked rice
½ medium green bell pepper, diced
½ medium red bell pepper, diced
¼ cup sliced scallions
¼ cup freshly grated Romano cheese
Vinaigrette dressing (a recipe follows)

Prepare the vinaigrette and let it chill while you work on the other ingredients.

Bring a medium saucepan of water to a boil. Add the shelled peas and cook for 2 minutes; drain and rinse with cold water. Set aside.

Toast the pine nuts in a small, heavy, dry pan, stirring over medium heat until they turn golden—about 5 minutes. Cool.

Combine the rice, peppers, scallions, cheese, peas, and nuts. Mix well, then drizzle on the dressing. Toss thoroughly to coat. Chill if not serving immediately, but try to eat this salad at room temperature.

Vinaigrette Dressing

¼ cup olive oil
2 tablespoons wine vinegar
1 teaspoon lemon juice
1 clove garlic, minced
¼ teaspoon dry mustard
¼ teaspoon dried oregano, crushed
Pinch each of basil and thyme (use fresh if available; minced fine)

Combine all ingredients in a jar. Cover and shake well. Refrigerate.

Darrel's Stir-Fried Chicken

Darrel Bowen works on a farm in Marengo, Illinois, which grows literally hundreds of different fruits and vegetables for sale at farmers markets.

Serves 4

2 whole chicken breasts, skinned and boned
1½ cups broth, made with 1 chicken and 1 beef bouillon cube
⅔ cup white wine
1 tablespoon soy sauce
1 teaspoon minced fresh ginger
½ teaspoon minced garlic

1 tablespoon cornstarch
½ cup water
Vegetable or peanut oil, as needed
2 quarter-size slices fresh ginger
1 cup broccoli florets
1 cup chopped peppers (a mixture of green, yellow, and red)
1 scallion, sliced (including some of the green part)
1 cup snow peas, trimmed

Cut the chicken into bite-size pieces. Darrel suggests placing the meat in the freezer for a few minutes to make the slicing easier.

Mix the broth, wine, soy sauce, ginger, and garlic in a shallow, nonmetallic dish. Add the chicken pieces and marinate for 20 minutes. Drain, saving the liquid.

Mix the cornstarch and water; set aside.

Heat a wok or large frying pan over a high flame. Add a little oil and stir-fry the ginger pieces until golden. Remove them and discard.

Stir-fry the vegetables separately, placing them in a bowl as you finish each and adding more oil as needed.

Cook the chicken pieces just until no more pink shows. Add the vegetables and reserved marinade; mix well. Stir in the cornstarch mixture; toss to combine. Cover and cook a minute or two, until the sauce has thickened and the mixture is thoroughly heated. Serve hot, over rice or chow mein noodles.

Shrimp and Snow Peas

This stir-fried mixture is gorgeous and likewise tasty.

Serves 4

1½ teaspoon cornstarch
2 teaspoons rice wine (or sherry)
½ teaspoon soy sauce
¼ cup peanut oil
2 medium cloves garlic, minced
½ medium onion, chopped
⅓ pound snow peas, trimmed
1 pound large shrimp, shelled and deveined
½ cup well-flavored chicken stock
Hot cooked rice

Stir together the cornstarch, wine, and soy sauce and set beside the pan along with the other ingredients.

Add the oil to the hot pan and toss in the onion and garlic. Stir and cook for about a minute, until both have started to soften. Add the snow peas and stir for about 30 seconds. Toss in the shrimp and continue to stir-fry until it is firm and pink. Turn down the flame to medium and add the stock and the cornstarch mixture. Stir and cook for about 2 minutes, until the sauce is thickened. Serve immediately, over rice.

Peppers

Along with the farmer's great thundering tide of fresh goods comes a rainbow array of peppers, ranging in vengeance from a luscious, thirst-quenching crunch to a nasal-clearing, throat-searing snap. They come in all colors, and their hues tell you precious little of the fire within. Some red peppers are quite sweet and mild, while others can make your temples perspire. Green and yellow peppers likewise run the gamut of heat.

Powerhouses of vitamin C, peppers team well with a huge variety of other foods and have been known to appear in soups, stews, salads, breads, and hors d'oeuvres—to say nothing of meat and vegetable dishes. And they provide a great edible bowl for your favorite stuffing mixtures.

So take your pick. You can find peppers at the market ranging from softball-size bell varieties to tiny hot peppers, no bigger than a baby's pinky. Generally the former are sweet, the latter more fiery, but don't take my word for it. Ask the grower for specifics. (Remember, when you're at the farmers market, the person behind the table is the last word.)

To pick a peck of peppers—or less—look for shiny, relatively heavy specimens. Those that seem lightweight for their size probably are dehydrated. The walls should be firm and the meat brightly colored. If the peppers are pale, wilted, flabby, or pockmarked with watery spots, they are too old. It is also likely that their stores of vitamin C are considerably depleted.

In preparing hot peppers, keep in mind that most of the heat is centralized in the inner ribs and seeds. Take them out when you core the pepper, and you'll have tamed the spicy beast significantly.

One of the best ways to highlight the pepper's inherent virtues is to roast it. Simply place it under a hot broiler, above searing white coals or, impaled on a fork, over an open gas flame. Toast it, turning often, until the skin is evenly blackened. Pop the pepper into a plain brown bag, crimp down the top, and let it steam itself out of its skin. After 10 or 15 minutes, take it out and pull off the skin, with the aid of a paring knife.

Prepared this way, a sweet pepper is ready to crown your best pizza or embellish your favorite skewered grill entree. And a peeled hot pepper can be stuffed and baked for a zesty treat.

One final note: when peeling hot peppers, be sure to wear rubber gloves. If you haven't any, make a point of washing your hands several times after you've finished, using lots of soap and water, before you touch your eyes or nose or pick up the baby.

On The Cutting Edge

Dealing with fresh produce demands using the right tools. And foremost among the requisite paraphernalia are knives. For your own safety and convenience as well as to reap optimum rewards for your efforts, it is crucial to use the right knife. You can't peel an apple with a chef's knife—at least, not without jeopardizing your future as the owner of ten fingers. And a paring knife won't chop onions nearly as proficiently as a big cleaver or chef's knife.

Keep your knives sharp. Not only will they make cleaner cuts and thinner slices when they're well honed, they'll also be less of a hazard to your digits. A dull knife requires much more downward pressure than a sharp blade, so it is more likely to slip when cutting. And a gash made by a dull knife seems to hurt more and take longer to heal than the good clean cut inflicted by a sharp knife.

The best edge can be found on knives made of carbon steel or high-carbon stainless steel. The former are the sharpest, but their chief drawback is their propensity for rust. Particularly sensitive to citrus fruits, onions, and tomatoes, carbon steel knives must be wiped dry after each use, or they will be left with dark stains. Sometimes the stained areas leak off flavors and discoloration back onto foods they later cut.

High-carbon stainless steel knives, while not as keenly sharp as their stainable counterparts, are a more practical choice for many people. They can be honed when they become dull, and they remain relatively undaunted by high-acid foods.

Beware of any knife that describes itself as never needing to be sharpened. That simply means that the blade is of such a hard metal that it cannot be sharpened, and it is doomed to a lifetime of dull cutting.

Curried Chicken-Stuffed Peppers

This is a beautiful dish with red peppers, but you may use green ones if you like.

Serves 4

4 large, rounded red or green bell peppers
1½ cups chicken stock
1 dried red pepper pod (optional)
2 whole chicken breasts, skinned and boned
¼ cup butter
1–2 teaspoons curry powder
½ large onion, chopped
1 medium tart apple (like a Granny Smith)
3 tablespoons flour
Salt to taste
¼ cup dried currants
¼ cup unsweetened coconut
1 hard-boiled egg, chopped fine
¼ cup chopped peanuts
Hot rice

Preheat the oven to 350°F.

Cut the tops off the peppers. Remove membranes and seeds. Drop into a kettle of boiling water for 2 minutes; rinse with cool water and invert on a rack to drain.

Heat the chicken stock and pepper pod in a large skillet. Put in the chicken breasts, cover and poach very gently just until firm, about 8–10 minutes. Remove from the broth; strain and reserve liquid. Cut the chicken into bite-size pieces and set aside.

Melt the butter in a medium saucepan over a gentle flame. Stir in the curry and cook for a minute or two. Sauté the onions and apple slowly until tender. Stir in the flour; cook for 2–3 minutes. Add the strained poaching liquid and salt and increase the heat to medium. Stir and cook until thickened. Stir in the currants, coconut, egg, and chicken. Mix well and divide between the four peppers. Set the peppers in a shallow baking dish with 1 inch of water in the bottom. Cover with the foil and bake at 350°F for 40–45 minutes or until thoroughly heated. Serve hot, sprinkled with peanuts and nestled in a mound of rice.

Three-Pepper Pizza

Simple, tasty, and a bit whimsical, this pizza has a yeast crust which doesn't make you wait around for it to rise.

Serves 4–6

½ green bell pepper
½ red bell pepper
½ yellow bell pepper
1 package (1 tablespoon) active dry yeast
¾ cup warm water
1½ teaspoons oil
1 tablespoon sugar
½ teaspoon salt
½ teaspoon garlic powder (optional)
2½–3 cups unbleached white flour
Oil
Sesame seeds
4–6 ounces smoked Gruyère cheese, sliced thin
1 tablespoon chopped fresh basil

Cut the curved portions off the peppers and reserve for another use. Cut the remaining portions into three oblong-shaped pieces. Roast the pepper pieces under the broiler or over a gas flame until charred. Place in a paper bag for 10–15 minutes, then pull off skins. Cut each oblong into two triangles; set aside.

Preheat the oven to 425°F.

Dissolve the yeast in the water; add the oil, sugar, salt, garlic powder, and 1 cup of the flour. Mix thoroughly. Add enough additional flour to make a soft dough. Knead until smooth and elastic. Lightly oil a 14-inch pizza pan; sprinkle with sesame seeds. Roll out the dough to fit the pan. Place it in the pan and put on the cheese slices. Sprinkle on the basil, then arrange the peppers in a flower-like pattern, alternating them by color, on top. Bake the pizza for 15–20 minutes in a 425-degree oven, until the crust is golden brown.

Ragout of Shrimp with Three Peppers

An easy and elegant company dish, this mixture pleases the eye as well as the palate.

Serves 6–8

1 medium onion, chopped
½ each: green, yellow, and red bell peppers, julienned
2 cloves garlic, minced
¼ cup butter
3 tablespoons flour
1 cup chicken stock, heated
¼ cup dry vermouth
2 tablespoons tomato paste
1 tablespoon chopped dill weed
Salt and pepper to taste
2 pounds cooked shrimp
1 cup sour cream
¼ cup chopped parsley
Hot rice

Sauté the onion, peppers, and garlic in butter until the onion is tender. Stir in the flour; cook for a minute or so. Add the hot stock; stir until thickened. Mix in the vermouth, tomato paste, dill, salt, and pepper. Simmer, covered, for about 5 minutes. Add the shrimp, sour cream, and parsley and heat through. Serve hot, over rice.

Salsa Fresca

This zippy, peppered-with-peppers "raw sauce" should be made several hours in advance, but not too far ahead of serving time. You want the flavors to blend without giving them a chance to fade. If possible, serve the salsa as a dip with tortilla chips you've made yourself by deep-frying quartered corn tortillas in hot oil. Yum!

Makes about 3 cups

1 16-ounce can tomatoes, drained and chopped
½ large fresh tomato, peeled and chopped fine
2–3 green onions, sliced (include some of the green part)
1–2 cloves garlic, minced
1–2 small green hot peppers, minced
⅓ cup chopped green bell pepper
2 tablespoons finely chopped peeled cucumber
2 mild green chiles, about 1″ × 6″ inches, roasted, peeled, and
    diced (if unavailable, substitute one 4-ounce can chopped
    green chiles)
3 tablespoons chopped fresh cilantro
1 tablespoon snipped chives
2 teaspoons coarse or Kosher salt
1 tablespoon fresh lime juice

Mix all the ingredients together in a glass or ceramic bowl. Cover and chill several hours. Bring to room temperature before serving.

Summer Squash

What would summer be without the vegetable that bears its name? The scourge of the home gardener, summer squash is the quintessential crop of plenty. From one small plant the squash blooms forth in copious glory, sometimes taking over the entire garden.

But that prolificacy makes the summer squashes—zucchini, yellow squash, and patty pan—natural members of the market collection. From late June onward, these versatile vegetables appear, in great quantities and with comforting predictability, on the farmer's table each week.

Summer squashes amount to embryonic gourds, harvested early in their development while the seeds and skins are edible. They provide valuable amounts of potassium and vitamins A and C.

Because they have such a high moisture content, you might want to drain some of the water out of your zucchini or other squash before cooking it. Simply slice, dice, or shred the squash, spread it out in a large colander and sprinkle it lightly with salt. Leave the squash for 30 minutes or so, then, gently squeeze out the excess moisture with your hands. If you plan to mix the squash into a baked or sautéed dish, this extra step will help to ensure a firmer, more flavorful, less soggy outcome.

At the market, look for firm, glossy, unblemished skin on your summer squash. They should feel heavy for their size. With yellow squash and zucchini, the smallest ones are really best, with their tender flesh and seeds and delicate flavor. They are also most attractive and manageable at this point, ready to be halved lengthwise and stir-fried as is, or perhaps sliced and mixed into a summer-vegetable medley. Of course, if you're planning to stuff the squash, you'll want to find larger ones. But be aware that very large (more than 8 inches long), overaged squashes probably will have thick skins, tough seeds, and dry, stringy flesh.

The pale green, scalloped-edged squashes known as patty pan varieties also are best when harvested small—try for a diameter of about 3 inches.

In all of these squashes, avoid dull, hard skins. The surface should be easy to pierce with your thumbnail, suggesting that the inside of the vegetable is still immature.

Summer Squash Salad

A colorful sampling of the farmer's offerings.

Serves 6

1 large or 2 medium yellow summer squash, quartered
  lengthwise and sliced
4 tomatoes, cut into wedges
1 green pepper, cut into strips
½ cup chopped green onions
¼ cup chopped parsley
2 tablespoons chopped basil
¾ cup vegetable oil
½ cup white wine vinegar
1 clove garlic, minced
1 teaspoon sugar
Salt and pepper to taste

Combine the squash, tomatoes, green pepper, onions, parsley, and basil in a large bowl. Put the oil, vinegar, garlic, sugar, salt, and pepper into a jar. Cover and shake well. Drizzle over the vegetables and toss gently. Chill well before serving.

Mom's Zucchini Medley

This thoroughly flexible recipe comes from my mother. The only rigid rules are the inclusion of zucchini, fresh tomatoes, and garlic salt. Layer into an ungreased casserole or soufflé dish, in amounts to suit the number you're feeding.

Zucchini, unpeeled, cut into 1-inch cubes
Green vegetables (broccoli, beans, peas)
Fresh mushrooms, sliced (optional)
Fresh tomatoes, sliced
Garlic salt
Sliced or grated cheese of your choosing
Strips of bacon (uncooked)

Preheat oven at 350°F.
   Layer everything evenly, then tuck in the ends of the zucchini around the edges of the dish. Bake for about 35–40 minutes at 350°F, until the bacon is done. Serve hot.

Angie's Stuffed Zucchini

My stepmother-in-law invented this hearty mixture.

Serves 4

2 large zucchini
½ pound ground beef
½ medium onion, chopped
2 tablespoons chopped parsley
1 teaspoon oregano
½ teaspoon salt
¼ teaspoon pepper
⅓ cup grated Romano cheese
½ cup grated cheddar cheese
¾ cup fine, dry bread crumbs
1 cup well-seasoned tomato sauce

Preheat the oven to 350°F.

Halve the zucchini and scoop out the innards, leaving a wall ½ inch thick all around. Dice the flesh and put it into a large bowl. Put the shells into a shallow baking dish or casserole.

Brown the beef with the onion; drain off any excess fat.

Combine the diced squash with the beef mixture, then stir in the parsley, oregano, salt, pepper, about half of the Romano, the cheddar, crumbs, and about ⅓ of the tomato sauce. Mix well, then spoon into the shells. Spread the remaining tomato sauce over the tops, then sprinkle with the remaining Romano cheese. Bake at 350°F for 30 minutes. Serve hot.

Frittata of Summer Squash

Simply a low-maintenance omelette, a frittata is a perfect way to enjoy the subtle flavor of summer squash.

Serves 3–4

2 tablespoons butter
¼ cup chopped onion
1 clove garlic, minced
2 cups diced zucchini or yellow squash
½ teaspoon thyme
¼ teaspoon marjoram
6 eggs
1 tablespoon milk
Parmesan cheese, grated fresh

Melt the butter in a medium-size skillet. Add the onion and garlic and sauté over moderate heat until translucent. Stir in the squash and herbs and continue to sauté the mixture, stirring often, until the squash is barely tender.

Beat the eggs with the milk in a small bowl. Spread the vegetables out evenly in the skillet and pour the eggs carefully over them. Cover the pan and turn the heat way down. Cook the frittata for 15–20 minutes, until the top is just set.

Place a large plate over the pan and invert it, dropping the mixture onto the plate. Slide the frittata carefully back into the pan and cook the other side for about 10 minutes, or until done. Remove from the pan and sprinkle with Parmesan cheese. Serve at room temperature.

Double Chocolate Zucchini Cake

Perfect for picnics, this cake needs no frosting. And it doesn't taste like squash.

Serves 10–12

½ cup softened margarine
½ cup vegetable oil
1¾ cups sugar
2 eggs
1 teaspoon vanilla
½ cup buttermilk
2½ cups unbleached white flour
¼ cup cocoa
½ teaspoon baking powder
1 teaspoon baking soda
½ teaspoon cinnamon
½ teaspoon ground cloves
2 cups finely diced zucchini (unpeeled)
⅓ cup semisweet chocolate chips

Preheat the oven to 325°F. Grease and flour a 9″ × 13″ pan.

Cream the margarine, oil, and sugar in a large bowl. Add the eggs, vanilla, and buttermilk; blend with an electric mixer until smooth, about one minute. Mix all the dry ingredients together and add to the creamed mixture; mix well. Stir in the diced zucchini.

Pour the batter into the prepared pan and sprinkle the chocolate chips over the top.

Bake at 325°F for about 45 minutes, until a toothpick inserted in the center comes out clean. Cool on a wire rack.

Tomatoes

Several years back, a song was released whose lyrics suggested that, in the end, true love and homegrown tomatoes are the only two items which money can't buy. I won't argue the point, but a close approximation of the latter item is indeed for sale at the farmers market. Plump, crimson-hued and inviting, local farm-grown tomatoes are one of summer's blazing triumphs.

Though they'll often make a first appearance sometime in early summer, tomatoes seem to peak around the time when the season's shadows begin to grow long, when so many other crops also are at an annual pinnacle. And many of them seem to pair well with that plump ruby fresh off the rambling vine, the tomato.

If you opt for perfectly ripe tomatoes at the market, plan to eat them—or put them up in jars, cans, or freezer containers—within a day. If you're buying a week's worth of household tomatoes, it makes more sense to choose individual fruits (yes, tomatoes are a citrus fruit) in varying stages of ripeness. Leave them on the counter, away from direct sunlight but handy for daily inspection, so you can eat (or refrigerate) them as they achieve prime edibility.

Do remember, though, that refrigerating tomatoes reduces their quality and inspires some mushiness, so plan to eat them the minute they become ripe, if you can. Once you've eaten your fill, and refrigerated even more, you may find you've overestimated your capacity (though not your love) for tomatoes. Rather than let them overripen, pop some into a plastic bag and freeze them as is. Use them when winter comes and you're making hearty soups, stews and sauces. Just run the frozen tomato under warm water, slip off the skin, core it, and chop it into your mixture.

At the market, look for reasonably unblemished, firm tomatoes with smooth skins and a nice rounded shape. Fully ripe ones will yield slightly to the gentle pressure of your hand and will have a deep red cast to them. Light-colored marks around the stem are harmless and sometimes even signal superior flavor. But do avoid tomatoes with deep growth cracks on top, as well as those showing splotches of yellow or green.

All-green tomatoes, on the other hand, can be a thing of delight. Unlike their temperamental scarlet cousins, green tomatoes will keep well for a couple of weeks if stored at about 50 degrees. They are a novel treat when made into sauces and relishes.

Some people like to reduce tomatoes to the tasty pulp, editing out the skin, seeds, and juice. To do this, either plunge them into boiling water for about 30 seconds, then into a bowl of ice water, or impale them on a fork and toast over a brisk gas flame until their skins split. Then simply pull off the skins, scoop out the seeds and juice with a teaspoon, and chop up the sweet tomato meat.

This reduction to the pulp is often done for tomatoes being preserved via canning or freezing. The seeds are difficult to remove after preserving, and some people find that they take on a slight bitterness after lengthy simmering.

The Soup Bag

Among the bonuses of cooking fresh vegetables is the debris you cut off. Far from being garbage, the ends and peelings are flavorful little nuggets which can team up to make rich and tasty soup stocks. I like to collect scraps in a "soup bag," a recloseable plastic bag kept in the freezer. When I pull the skin off of an onion, trim the root end from a piece of celery, peel a potato, or defoliate a sprig of parsley, the portions being removed go directly into the bag. When the bag is full, it's time to make soup. You can use the scraps with meat or poultry bones, or all alone, for an intriguing vegetable stock. Almost everything the farmer sells is suitable for soup. Do avoid eggplant trimmings, however, as they can produce a bitter stock. Beyond that, nearly anything goes. Try the trimmings from the vegetables you usually use for stock, then experiment with those not usually thought of as soup stuff: green pepper stems, broccoli stalks and leaves, zucchini ends, tomato skins, pea pods, scallion tops, spinach stems, empty corn cobs, lettuce cores, apple peels, bean strings . . . you decide where to draw the line.

Gazpacho

This chilled soup is flavorful, easy to prepare, and plenty festive for company. The process of garnishing lends the air of a curry feast.

Serves 6

4 large, ripe tomatoes, chopped
1 large cucumber, peeled, seeded, and diced
½ cup chopped red onion
1–2 cloves garlic, minced
¼ cup chopped watercress
½ medium green pepper, chopped
1 tablespoon chopped basil
3 tablespoons olive oil
2 tablespoons red wine vinegar
2 cups cold tomato juice
1 teaspoon salt
¼ teaspoon cumin
3–4 drops Tabasco
A few grains cayenne pepper
1 teaspoon honey
Pepper to taste
Garnishes: chopped scallions, hard-boiled eggs, homemade croutons

Put the tomatoes, cucumber, onion, garlic, watercress, green pepper, and basil into a large bowl and mix well. Ladle half of the mixture into a blender or food processor and puree. Return to the bowl and mix thoroughly. Whisk in the olive oil, vinegar, tomato juice, and seasonings. Taste and adjust seasonings, if necessary. Chill for several hours.

Pass the garnishes in bowls as you serve.

Tabouli

This filling Middle Eastern salad is chock full of nutritious foods. And it's quite tasty, too.

Serves 8

1 cup dried bulgur wheat
1½ teaspoons salt
1½ cups boiling water
¼ cup fresh lemon juice
2 medium cloves garlic, minced
¼ cup olive oil
2 medium tomatoes, diced
½ cup scallions, sliced (include some green)
1 medium cucumber, peeled, seeded, and chopped
1 teaspoon chopped fresh mint
½ cup chopped parsley
Pepper to taste
2–3 ounces feta cheese

Combine the bulgur and salt in a large bowl. Pour the boiling water over it and cover for 15–20 minutes, until the water is absorbed. The wheat should be chewy.

Add the lemon juice, garlic, and olive oil; toss thoroughly. Chill for 2–3 hours.

Stir in the vegetables, herbs, and pepper just before serving. Crumble the feta over the top and serve cold.

Egg and Tomato Bake

Great for brunch.

Serves 6

2 medium tomatoes, peeled
6 slices bread
6 hard-cooked eggs, sliced
2 tablespoons butter
2 tablespoons flour
1 cup milk
¼ teaspoon dry mustard
A few grains cayenne pepper
Salt and pepper to taste
¾ cup grated sharp cheddar cheese
12 strips thin-sliced bacon, cooked crisp and crumbled
Chopped parsley

Preheat the oven to 350°F.

Cut each tomato crosswise into three slices. Toast the bread lightly.

Using a large casserole or individual oven-proof dishes, arrange sliced egg on each piece of toast, top with a slice of tomato and bake at 350°F for 15 minutes.

Meanwhile, make the cheese sauce: melt the butter in a small saucepan. Stir in the flour and cook, stirring, for a minute or two. Stir in the milk and seasonings. Cook over moderate heat, stirring still, until thickened. Add the cheese gradually and stir until it melts. Remove from heat.

Spoon the hot sauce over the hot tomato slices and return to the oven until the sauce begins to bubble, about 10–15 minutes. Remove from the oven, surround each serving with a ring of bacon bits and sprinkle parsley over the top. Serve immediately.

Minestrone

When the weather turns cruel, you might want a hot soup. This mixture can even be made with the frozen surplus from those long-ago summer days.

Serves 10–12

1 pound ripe tomatoes
1 large onion, chopped
2 ribs celery, sliced
¼ cup olive oil
4 cups beef broth (preferably homemade)
2 medium zucchini
1 24-ounce can Great Northern beans
1 cup dry elbow macaroni
1 cup finely shredded cabbage
½ cup chopped parsley
1–2 cloves garlic, minced
¼ teaspoon pepper

Bring a couple of quarts of water to a boil in a large kettle. Drop in the fresh tomatoes and leave for about 30–40 seconds. Drain and plunge into a bowl of ice water. (If using frozen tomatoes, just run under warm tap water and pull off the skins.) Peel off the skins, remove the cores, and chop coarsely. Place in a bowl, with their juice, and set aside.

In a large saucepan, sauté the onion and celery in the olive oil until soft. Add the broth, an equal amount of water, the tomatoes, zucchini, beans, macaroni, cabbage, parsley, garlic, and pepper. Bring to a boil, reduce the heat, and simmer for 30 minutes. Serve hot, with a crusty loaf of bread.

Marinated Tomato Salad

This simple formula describes one of the very best ways to enjoy the flavor of perfectly ripe tomatoes. You should allow about half a large tomato per person.

In an attractive, shallow dish, layer:

Sliced tomatoes
Sliced onions (the sweeter the better)
Salt, pepper, and a pinch of sugar
1 teaspoon minced fresh basil
1 teaspoon olive oil
1 teaspoon wine vinegar

Refrigerate for at least 2 hours before serving.

Green Tomato Chutney

Makes about 4 pints

8 pounds green tomatoes, chopped
2 cups chopped green pepper
1 cup chopped onion
1½ cups sugar
1¼ cups cider vinegar
4 teaspoons salt
1 tablespoon dry mustard
1 tablespoon mustard seed
1½ teaspoons celery seed
1 teaspoon turmeric

Combine all of the ingredients in a large, heavy-bottomed, non-aluminum saucepan. Place over medium heat and stir until the sugar is dissolved. Increase heat and cook briskly for 25 minutes, stirring often to prevent the mixture from sticking to the bottom of the pan.

Ladle into hot, sterilized jars, filling to within ½ inch of the top. Cover with clean lids and process in a boiling water bath for 15 minutes. Cool, label, and store.

The Weirdos

Certain staples form the foundation of the farmer's fare. Squash and tomatoes, peas and potatoes are among those crops which can be found at virtually any outdoor produce market at some point during the growing season.

But occasionally you stumble across a curious crop, something you may have never seen before and are not likely to find in a conventional supermarket. Here is where you discover golden and albino beets, tender and sweetly flavored; tiny potatoes, no bigger than marbles; a plethora of squashes, including their beautiful and delectable blossoms; gorgeous heads of vibrant purple cauliflower; yellow pear tomatoes; tangy tart cherries, and tiny bite-size plums. Watch for these goodies. They can treat the palate and tickle the imagination.

But do ask the farmer about them. He may have good ideas for using them most deliciously, or he may even have a little tidbit of vegetable trivia which will enlighten you. It's important to remember to avail yourself of the grower's expertise—it's one of your best market resources.

Sautéed Golden Beets

Simple and unusual, this dish is worlds away from the pickled red disks packed in jars and sold in the supermarket.

Serves 4

6 medium (3-inch diameter) golden beets
1 tablespoon lemon juice
3 tablespoons butter
2 teaspoons chopped sweet marjoram
Salt and pepper

Scrape the beets and grate coarsely into a medium bowl. Sprinkle with lemon juice and toss gently.

   Melt the butter in a skillet. Add the beets and sauté, stirring often, until they are just tender, about five minutes. Sprinkle with marjoram, season to taste, and serve hot.

Baby Potato Salad

Not the usual drowned-in-mayonnaise mixture.

Serves 6–8

1½ pound tiny potatoes (red- or brown-skinned)
2 medium ribs celery, diced
½ red onion, chopped
¼ cup balsamic vinegar
¼ cup olive oil
¼ cup vegetable oil
12–14 basil leaves, chopped
1 tablespoon chopped dill
1 teaspoon Dijon mustard
1 clove garlic, minced
Salt and pepper to taste
½ cup radish sprouts

Bring a large kettle of lightly salted water to a boil. Add the potatoes and cook until tender but not mushy, about 10 minutes. Drain and place in a large bowl. Add the celery and onion and mix well. Let the mixture cool to room temperature.

   Combine the vinegar, oils, herbs, mustard, garlic, salt, and pepper. Blend thoroughly, then pour over the vegetables in the bowl. Toss to coat. Chill.

   At serving time, sprinkle with the sprouts and serve cold.

Purple Cauliflower Salad

Easy, eye-pleasing, and packed with protein and vitamin A.

Serves 6

1 medium head purple cauliflower, separated into florets
1 cup Miracle Whip
¼ cup freshly grated Parmesan cheese
2 tablespoons sugar
2 strips bacon, cooked crisp and crumbled

Bring a kettle of lightly salted water to a boil. Add the cauliflower and cook for 2 minutes. Drain and plunge into ice water to stop the cooking process. Drain and pat dry. Place in a large bowl.

In a small bowl, combine the Miracle Whip, Parmesan cheese, and sugar. Spoon over the cauliflower and toss to coat. Chill. Sprinkle with bacon before serving.

Stuffed Squash Blossoms Tempura

Fabulous finger food, these nummies should be eaten right after cooking to maximize their crispness and delicate flavor.

Serves 4–5

12–15 squash blossoms
2 eggs, separated
¼ teaspoon salt
¾ cup warm water
1 tablespoon vegetable oil
¾ cup flour
1 cup shredded sharp cheddar cheese
12–15 4-inch pieces of scallion tops
Oil for deep frying

Wash the blossoms and trim stems to about 1 inch. Place in a bowl of ice water and refrigerate.

Beat the egg yolks, salt, water, and oil together. Stir in the flour gradually; beat until smooth. Let the batter sit for an hour or so to allow the flour to expand, making a lighter result.

Beat the egg whites until soft peaks form. Fold into the batter.

Remove the blossoms from the water; pat dry with paper towels. Spoon about a tablespoon of cheese into the middle of each, then gather up the petals to enclose the cheese. Gently tie the petals shut with pieces of scallion tops.

Heat the oil in a large saucepan or wok to about 365°F. Lightly coat the stuffed blossoms with the batter. Fry them, three or four at a time, until golden brown and crisp, turning several times. Drain the blossoms and serve hot.

Pasta-and-Produce Mergers: That's Using Your Noodle

The goods available at the farmers market, taken en masse, are arguably adequate for a full and balanced diet all by themselves, at least for the duration of the harvest. Corn and peas are just two among many sources of complex carbohydrates offered by the farmer. Beans of many colors are there for protein; leafy green vegetables provide iron and minerals; broccoli, tomatoes, and strawberries contribute vitamin C. Really, there's little more a person could want.

But when you combine fresh produce with another food—something equally wholesome, delicious, and versatile—you create a partnership. Take pasta, for example. When made from hard durum wheat or semolina, it's a good source of protein and carbohydrates all by itself. Mix it with some vegetables, or even fruit, and it's a match made in heaven. It's Al Dente Moves to the Farm. It's a meal.

More than just salad, pasta-and-produce pairings are a sensible, delectable way to have it all. Well, almost.

Fresh Tomato-Mozzarella Sauce

A simple, piquant mélange of market flavors, this sauce promises to glorify a forlorn plate of linguine beyond its wildest hopes.
Enough for about ¾ pound of pasta

3 large, ripe tomatoes
2–3 tablespoons chopped basil
1 large clove garlic, minced
Pepper to taste
6 ounces mozzarella cheese, cut into ½-inch cubes

Coarsely chop the tomatoes; mince the basil leaves. Combine everything in a glass or ceramic bowl and let the flavors blend for an hour or so. Serve at room temperature, over hot pasta.

Vermicelli with Broccoli-Garlic Sauce

Colorful and redolent of garlic, this dish is a meal in itself.
Serves 6

1 large bunch broccoli
2 tablespoons olive oil
¼ cup butter
2–3 cloves garlic, minced
1 cup half & half
1 teaspoon salt
Pepper to taste
½ cup freshly grated Parmesan cheese
1 pound vermicelli, cooked and drained

Cut the broccoli into flowerets, including some of the thinner stalks. Steam quickly, until barely tender; chop fairly fine. Heat the oil and butter in a large saucepan; add garlic and cook over low heat for about 2 minutes. Stir in cream, salt, and pepper. Heat until almost bubbling, then add broccoli and Parmesan cheese. Cover, take off the heat, and let sit for a couple of minutes to blend the flavors. Toss with freshly cooked pasta and serve hot, with additional cheese if desired.

Fettucine with Chicken and Asparagus

An early-season treat.

Serves 3–4

1 whole chicken breast, skinned and boned
½ pound fresh asparagus
2 tablespoons butter
3 scallions, sliced
Salt and pepper to taste
¾ cup half & half
Pinch of cayenne
Pinch of nutmeg
3 ounces Swiss cheese, shredded
¾ pound freshly cooked fettucine
Parmesan cheese

Cut the chicken into bite-size strips and set aside.

Peel the outer skin off the stem end of the larger asparagus spears. Slice the spears diagonally at 1-inch intervals. Drop into a pan of boiling water; let cook for just 60 seconds. Drain well and set aside.

Melt the butter in a large skillet over medium–high heat. Toss in the scallions and chicken, stirring until the chicken loses its pinkness—about 60 seconds. Add salt and pepper to taste; gently stir in the asparagus, and sauté about 30 seconds more. Mix in the cream, cayenne, and nutmeg. Blend well, then add the Swiss cheese. Cook and stir until cheese melts. Add pasta, toss, and serve. Pass Parmesan cheese separately.

Tortellini-Pesto Primavera

Colorful and bursting with fresh flavor.

Serves 3–4

4 ounces dry tortellini
1 small stalk broccoli
1 small zucchini, julienned
¼ medium yellow bell pepper
2 tablespoons chopped red onion
1 medium carrot, julienned
1 medium tomato, peeled, seeded, juiced, and diced
Kernels from one cooked ear of corn
⅓ cup olive oil and vegetable oil (a blend)
1 tablespoon lemon juice
2 tablespoons white wine vinegar
2 tablespoons pesto
1 clove garlic, minced
Salt and pepper to taste

Bring a large saucepan of lightly salted water to a boil. Add the tortellini and cook until al dente, about 20 minutes. Drain.

Cut the broccoli into small florets, including some of the thinner stalks. Drop into boiling water for 60 seconds; drain and add to the tortellini along with the zucchini, bell pepper, onion, carrot, tomato, and corn.

Combine the oils, lemon juice, vinegar, pesto, garlic, salt, and pepper in a small jar. Cover and shake vigorously for 30 seconds. Drizzle over the tortellini mixture and toss gently until well mixed. Serve chilled or at room temperature.

Fruit-Pasta Salad

Quite unusual, this mixture is perfect for a summer luncheon entree. Leftover dressing can be used with either fruit or vegetable salads.

Serves 3–4

6 ounces pasta, in small shapes (shells, corkscrews, mostaccioli, or other macaroni)
½ cup seedless grapes, halved if large
½ large cantaloupe, diced
2 large, tart apples, peeled and diced
1 teaspoon fresh lemon juice
1 cup sliced strawberries
1 cup blueberries
Celery Seed Dressing (recipe follows)

Cook the pasta until just done. Drain and set aside.

Combine the grapes, melon, and apples. Sprinkle on the lemon juice and toss gently. Mix in the pasta, then drizzle on the dressing to taste. Fold in the berries just before serving.

Celery Seed Dressing

Use this dressing on any fruit salad or drizzle it over crisp spinach leaves.

½ cup vegetable oil
¼ cup vinegar
½ cup catsup
1 cup powdered sugar
2 teaspoons celery seed
1 teaspoon Worcestershire sauce
Salt and pepper to taste

Combine all ingredients in a small bowl. Beat on high speed of mixer until thickened, about 2 minutes.

Parsley-Garlic Pasta

If you have a pasta machine, try this special dough. It's wonderful for lasagne or can be made into linguine or fettucine, to be tossed with just a coating of butter and some cheese.

Makes about a pound of pasta

2 cups semolina flour
½ teaspoon salt
3 eggs
1 tablespoon finely chopped garlic
½ cup chopped parsley, loosely packed

Mix the semolina and salt in a large bowl; make a well in the center. Put the eggs, garlic, and parsley in the well; mix together with a fork. Gradually work in the semolina to make a fairly stiff dough. Knead until the sticky feeling is gone, then process into shapes according to the directions that came with your machine.

CHAPTER 6
GOLDEN DAYS

As summer melts gradually into autumn, the harvest changes its look a bit. Though the market maintains its now-accustomed atmosphere of bountiful plenty, the goods have changed. All but gone are the tender, delicate young crops of early summer, replaced now by the robust flavors and deep, warm hues of the fall market. This is the time when winter squashes, grapes, pumpkins, apples, and root crops take center stage. The market becomes a place to go for solace, when the end of summer seems too close at hand, the nights a little too crisp. Looking at the treasures of the harvest, one suddenly feels things falling into place: so this is why there's autumn.

You go to the market to fill up on Mother Nature's sheer fecundity one last time, before winter gales make local fresh produce a mere figment of the memory. Yes, do get your fill.

A Hard-Headed Harvest

Foremost among the features of the fall market is the Gourd family, a thick-skulled bunch with brains that rattle. Well, maybe not literally. Winter squash and pumpkins are a late-season dividend, inspiring treats both sweet and savory—and, of course, spilling at overflow levels from the farmer's fields.

Pumpkins and winter squash, including acorn, butternut, Hubbard, and turban types, among many others, are all essentially squashes that have been allowed to ripen on the vine. Another variety—the yellow, green, and patty pan types known collectively as summer squash—are picked when immature, before their seeds and rind toughen beyond palatability.

These late-season squashes are nutritional giants among the vegetable set. They are an excellent source of vitamin A, potassium, and other minerals, Rich in fiber and complex carbohydrates, they cook up beautifully via numerous methods. But whether you bake, broil, grill, steam, or fry it, this hardy vegetable family spells worthwhile food.

In choosing squash, ask the grower about any varieties you don't recognize. You may discover yet another delicious market curiosity. In general, look for a hard, tough rind free of cuts and soft spots. A very tender rind probably means the squash is immature. It should look clean and feel heavy for its size. And check to make sure the severed stem is intact. The squash needs that stub to remain attached, to head off spoilage and moisture loss.

As for pumpkins, save the overgrown field specimens for carving into jack-o'-lanterns. They are likely to be stringy and watery inside. It's the smaller eating variety, sometimes called sugar pumpkins, that are best for cooking. Look for a nicely rounded shape, a good bright orange color and a firmly attached stem. The severed end should show evidence of being cut from the vine rather than torn. Snipping the stem creates less harvest trauma to the sweet meat within.

Baked Acorn Squash

Smooth and just slightly sweet, this easy side dish is a celebration of autumn flavors.

Serves 4

2 acorn squash
2 tablespoons butter, melted
½ cup unsweetened applesauce
2 tablespoons pure maple syrup
1 teaspoon finely grated fresh ginger

Preheat the oven to 375°F.

Halve the squash; scoop out the seeds. Combine the butter, applesauce, syrup, and ginger and distribute evenly among the halves. Set in a baking pan containing half an inch of hot water. Cover with foil and bake about an hour, or until tender.

Autumn Turkey Pie

A homey, one-dish meal, this pie offers great potential for your leftovers.

Serves 4–5

1 cup chopped onion
2 tablespoons butter
3 tablespoons flour
2 cups chicken or turkey broth
3 tablespoons lemon juice
¼ teaspoon thyme
A few drops Tabasco
2 cups diced cooked turkey
1½ cups diced cooked squash
1½ cups sliced cooked carrots
1 cup sliced celery, steamed until tender
2 tablespoons raisins
Pastry for a single 9-inch pie crust

In a medium skillet, sauté the onion in butter until golden. Sprinkle in the flour; cook and stir for a minute or two. Gradually stir in the broth; add lemon juice, thyme, and Tabasco. Cook, stirring constantly, until mixture boils and begins to thicken.

Preheat the oven to 400°F.

In a 6-cup casserole or baking dish, layer the turkey, squash, carrots, celery, and raisins. Pour the sauce carefully over all. Roll out the pastry to a size that suits your pan and cover the casserole with it, crimping around the edges. Slash the top in three places. Bake at 400°F for 30–35 minutes or until browned. Serve hot.

Farmer's Squash

A rich mixture suitable for any kind of winter squash.

Serves 6

3 pounds winter squash
¼ pound bacon
1 cup plain yogurt or sour cream
1 small onion, chopped
Salt and pepper to taste

Peel squash and cut in half. Remove the seeds and fibers; cut into cubes. Place in a pan, in a steamer if you have one, with about an inch of water in the bottom; steam for 20–30 minutes or until tender. Be careful not to let all of the water boil away.

Meanwhile, fry the bacon until crisp. Reserve the drippings and crumble the bacon. Preheat the oven to 400°F.

Drain the squash and mash it. Add the bacon, drippings, yogurt, onion, and seasonings; mix well. Spoon the mixture into an un-greased 1-quart casserole and bake for 20 minutes. Serve very hot.

Squash-Stuffed Mushrooms

This is a flexible hors d'oeuvre with a savory character, an offshoot of the Farmer's Squash recipe. If you use giant mushroom caps, it can be served as a first course or a side dish. You might want to try stuffing tomatoes instead of mushrooms, but be careful not to overbake them or they will collapse.

Serves 8

2 pounds winter squash
3 strips bacon
1 small onion, chopped fine
⅔ cup plain yogurt
½ cup freshly grated Parmesan cheese
Salt and pepper to taste
2 pounds mushrooms
2 tablespoons butter
1 cup fresh bread crumbs

Preheat the oven to 400°F.

Cut the squash in half. Peel it and cut into cubes. Bring about an inch of water to a boil in a large saucepan; add squash and steam until tender, about 20–30 minutes, keeping an eye on the water level as it steams. Drain the squash, mash it, and set aside.

Fry the bacon until crisp. Crumble and add, along with the drippings, to the squash. Add the onion, yogurt, Parmeasan cheese, salt, and pepper. Mix well.

Wipe the mushrooms with a damp cloth and carefully twist out the stem from each, leaving it hollow. Put the caps, in a single layer, into a baking dish. Spoon the squash mixture into a pastry bag and pipe it into the mushrooms, or use a teaspoon to fill them.

Melt the butter in a small skillet; toss in the crumbs and stir until the butter is absorbed. Sprinkle the crumbs over the stuffed mushrooms. Bake in 400°F oven for 10–15 minutes, until heated through.

Serve immediately.

A Pumpkin Full of Supper

The beautiful presentation and full flavor of this one-gourd meal belie its humble ingredients and the ease of its preparation.

Serves 4–6

1 tablespoon butter
1½ cups chopped celery
1 cup chopped onion
¼ pound mushrooms, wiped clean and sliced
1 pound hamburger
2 tablespoons soy sauce
2 tablespoons brown sugar
1 10¾-ounce can condensed cream of mushroom soup
1 tablespoon chopped thyme (or 1 teaspoon dried)
2 cups cooked rice
1 medium pumpkin

Preheat the oven to 350°F

Melt the butter in a medium-size skillet, and sauté the celery and onion in it until just tender. Add the mushrooms and cook just until the liquid is evaporated. Remove from the skillet to a large bowl.

In the same pan, brown the hamburger. Drain off any excess fat. Put the meat into the bowl with the vegetables, adding the soy sauce, brown sugar, soup, thyme, and rice. Mix well.

Cut the top off the pumpkin. Scoop out the insides, scraping well. Spoon the meat-rice mixture into the pumpkin. Replace the top and bake at 350°F for an hour. Serve immediately, scooping up a bit of cooked pumpkin flesh along with the rice mixture as you go.

Fresh Pumpkin Buttermilk Muffins

You needn't cook the daylights out of a pumpkin and then mash it silly in order to get the most from it. Try this fresh-grated form.

Makes 12 muffins

1 cup unbleached white flour
½ cup whole-wheat flour
½ cup sugar
1 teaspoon baking powder
½ teaspoon each: salt, cinnamon, and nutmeg
¼ cup unsalted butter, softened
1 beaten egg
½ cup buttermilk
1 cup grated fresh pumpkin (rind excluded)
½ cup chopped walnuts or pecans

Preheat the oven to 400°F.

Mix the flours, sugar, baking powder, salt, and spices. Add the remaining ingredients except the nuts, stirring only enough to moisten everything. Fold in the nuts.

Spoon the mixture into greased muffin tins, filling them ¾ of the way up. Bake at 400°F for 20 minutes.

Soy-Garlic Pumpkin Seeds

The oversized monster pumpkin you choose for a jack-o'-lantern may be unsuitable for eating, but its seeds are just fine for baking and nibbling.

Just scoop out the seeds and rinse them in a colander, separating out the stringy stuff. Pat dry on paper towels and put into a bowl with about 2 tablespoons of soy sauce and a minced clove of garlic. Marinate for about 30 minutes, then drain and pat dry again. Bake in a preheated 250-degree oven for 50–60 minutes or so, stirring once or twice, until almost white and dry. Spread out on paper towels to cool and crispen.

Pumpkin Yule Log

You don't have to wait for Christmas to enjoy this smooth and pleasantly spiced cake. But if you'd like to, your pumpkin will keep until then, seated in a cool, dry spot.

Serves 8–10

3 eggs
1 cup sugar
⅔ cup cooked pureed pumpkin
¾ cup unbleached white flour
1 teaspoon lemon juice
1 teaspoon grated lemon rind
2 teaspoons cinnamon
1 teaspoon baking powder
1 teaspoon ground ginger
½ teaspoon nutmeg
½ teaspoon salt
Cream Cheese Filling (recipe follows)

Preheat the oven to 350°F. Line a greased 10″ × 15″ jelly roll pan with wax paper, greasing the paper too.

Beat together the eggs, sugar, pumpkin, and flour. Gently mix in the lemon juice, rind, cinnamon, baking powder, ginger, nutmeg, and salt.

Pour the batter into the prepared pan, spreading it evenly. Bake at 350°F for 15 minutes. Immediately invert the pan onto a clean tea towel that has been sprinkled with powdered sugar. Roll up the cake lengthwise, towel and all; let cool. (Meanwhile, make the filling.)

Unroll the cake and spread the filling over it, leaving a ½-inch margin all around the edge. Roll up the cake again, without the towel this time. Wrap it in plastic and chill for at least 2 hours. Cut into 1-inch slices and serve.

Cream Cheese Filling

1 cup sifted powdered sugar
1 8-ounce package cream cheese, softened
¼ cup butter, softened
½ teaspoon vanilla

Beat together until smooth.

Pumpkin-Raisin Bread

A big, unusual loaf, great for breakfast toast or cream cheese sandwiches.

Makes 1 loaf

3¾–4¼ cups unbleached white flour, divided
1 package (1 tablespoon) active dry yeast
¼ cup sugar
½ teaspoon salt
½ teaspoon cinnamon
¼ teaspoon nutmeg
Pinch of cloves
¼ cup water
⅔ cup cooked pureed pumpkin
3 tablespoons butter
2 eggs
¾ cup raisins

In a large mixer bowl, combine 1½ cups of the flour, the yeast, sugar, salt, and spices. Set aside.

Heat the water, pumpkin, and butter in a small saucepan or in the microwave until warm, about 110°–120° (the butter doesn't need to melt). Add to the flour mixture, then add the eggs and beat at low speed until moistened. Beat at medium speed for 3 minutes. Using a big spoon, stir in the raisins and enough additional flour to make a firm dough. Knead on a generously floured surface for about 10 minutes, until smooth and elastic. Place in a greased bowl, turning once to coat the dough. Cover and let rise in a warm place until doubled in bulk, about an hour.

Preheat the oven to 375°F.

Punch down the dough. On a lightly floured surface, pat it out to a 7″×14″ rectangle. Starting with a short side, roll the dough up tightly, pinching the edges and ends to seal them. Place in a greased 9″×5″ loaf pan, cover and let rise in a warm place until almost doubled again.

Bake in a 375°F oven for about 45 minutes, until golden brown. If the loaf darkens too quickly, cover the top loosely with a piece of foil. The loaf is done when it makes a hollow sound when tapped on the bottom. Remove from the pan immediately and cool on its side on a wire rack.

This Little Baby Went To Market ...

Few place are better sources of baby food than the farmers market. Leave the jars of pureed goo on the supermarket shelf—you can do better.

Whether Baby is eating thin mushes or feeding herself chewy "finger foods," the market abounds with menu possibilities. Carrots, peas, squash, and sweet potatoes are there, ready to get the beginner started off on a lifetime of gustatory joys.

All you need do to prepare these foods—or virtually any of the fruits and vegetables sold at the market—is cook and mash them. Steaming retains the most vitamins and minerals, and the water you use for cooking can then be used to thin the finished mush. But if boiling seems a better way to deal with your chosen food, fine. You're still doing better than canned.

Once you've cooked the vegetable or fruit to full tenderness, puree it in a blender of food processor, to perfect smoothness for a novice eater or perhaps on the chunky side for a baby with new teeth to try out. Feed Baby his fill, then plop the leftovers onto a wax paper–covered cookie sheet, mounding them into serving-size piles, or pour them into a clean ice cube tray. Then freeze. Come January, a cube or two taken from the Deepfreeze, defrosted and gently warmed, will carry Baby back to the halcyon days of the harvest season.

You can defrost and warm your purees in the microwave or on the stovetop, maybe in one of those eggpoaching devices with the little round pits in them.

Of course, many fruits and vegetables are perfect finger foods as is. Asparagus, green beans, and corn are all interesting things to mouth, roll around on the high-chair tray, and fling onto the floor. With corn, you might want to run a paring knife down the center of each row of kernels, so baby can suck out the sweet stuff and leave the less digestible skins on the cob.

Berries are good self-feeding possibilities too, as are slices of apples, peaches, pears, and plums. Remove the peels if Baby isn't yet ready for them.

Latecomer Fruits

In the harvest there always seems to be a slowpoke or two. Not eager to brave the summer's heat, these crops hang back in favor of autumn's more temperate climes. Among these late arrivals are grapes and pears, two sweet jewels of the market's twilight days. When the fruits of late summer finally make their debut, you know Jack Frost cannot be far behind.

Few sights at the fall market are more sumptuous than a cluster of vine-fresh Concord grapes, little velvet spheres of deep violet intensity.

Look for firm, well-colored grapes that are securely attached to their stems. Avoid grapes with bleached areas around their stems, as well as leaking fruit, which probably is decayed.

You may have trouble finding seedless grapes at the farmers market, which makes pies and other fruit desserts an ambitious undertaking indeed. But do try some preparation that allows the seeds and skin of the grapes to be sieved out. Preserves are one good possibility; sauces are another.

Pears, like peaches and nectarines, usually are available at a not-quite-table-ready stage of ripeness. Plan to take them home and enjoy them for a few days as a still life, arranged attractively in a bowl and left on the counter or in the middle of the dinner table. As they ripen, wash them and either transfer them to the refrigerator or devour them without further ado.

At the market, choose pears that are firm, but not hard. Again, use the grower's expertise in discovering which varieties—and there are lots of them—are best for your purposes. The farmer may have such species of pears as Anjou or Comice, light green or yellowish in appearance; Bosc, gently russeted in shades of yellow; Bartletts, ranging from yellow to red; or the green-tinted Winter Nelis variety. Of course, there are many others.

Whatever the type, select fruit that is unblemished, well shaped, and clean. Pears that look shriveled, wilted, or waterlogged may have been picked too early and will never attain perfect ripeness.

Ideally, the fruit should feel as though it has just begun to soften. If you want to eat the pears right away, look for a slight tenderness around the stem end.

Most important, make it a point to savor the pears. They offer one final opportunity to enjoy a local form of the sweet, tender tastiness which all too soon will be merely a luscious memory.

Concord Grape Butter

Grape spreads don't have to be laced with heavy doses of sugar. Try this easy butter, as close to pure grapes-in-a-jar as you can get.

Makes 4 pints of butter

2 quarts Concord grapes
2 tablespoons water
Honey to taste

Put the grapes and water into a large, heavy-bottomed, nonaluminum saucepan. Heat, mashing the grapes. Cook over medium heat, stirring frequently, until thickened. Put through a food mill to remove the skins and seeds, then return to the pan and continue cooking until quite thick. Sweeten with honey as desired, then pack into hot, sterilized, pint-size jars to within ½ inch of the tops. Seal and process in a boiling water bath for 10 minutes. Cool, label, and store.

White Grape Jelly

A nonstaining version of a classic spread.

Makes about 3 half-pints

2 pounds white grapes
¼ cup water
2 cups sugar

Wash and stem the grapes. Place in a large, nonaluminum pot with the water. Bring to a boil, mashing the grapes against the sides of the pan. Reduce the heat and cook gently for 30–40 minutes, stirring occasionally. Put the mixture into a dampened jelly bag or into a strainer lined with cheesecloth and let drain for 2 hours.

Return the strained juice to the pan and bring to a boil. Add the sugar very gradually, maintaining the boil, and cook to 8 degrees above the boiling point as measured on your thermometer. Boil hard at this temperature for one minute longer. Remove from the heat. Skim foam from the top, then ladle into hot, sterilized half-pint jars to within half an inch of the tops. Seal and process for 10 minutes in a boiling water bath. Cool, label, and store.

Pear Bread

Makes one loaf

½ cup unsalted butter, softened
1 cup sugar
2 eggs
2 cups unbleached white flour
1 teaspoon baking powder
½ teaspoon salt
½ teaspoon baking soda
Pinch of nutmeg
¼ cup buttermilk
1 teaspoon vanilla
1 cup peeled, coarsely chopped pears
½ cup chopped walnuts or pecans

Preheat the oven to 350°F.

Cream the butter and sugar until fluffy. Add the eggs, beating after each one. Set aside.

Sift together the flour, baking powder, salt, soda, and nutmeg. Add the dry ingredients to the creamed mixture alternately with the buttermilk, stirring after each addition. Stir in the vanilla, pears, and nuts.

Pour the batter into a greased loaf pan. Bake at 350°F for about an hour, until the bread begins to pull away from the sides of the pan. Cool in the pan. Slice and serve slathered with butter, softened cream cheese, or apple butter.

CHAPTER 7

A BLIZZARD IN THE ORCHARD

As even the most ardent fan of summer sun and fun is apt to admit, there's something about fall that is worth looking forward to. It's not just the fabulous color show presented by the local forestry. It's more than the exhilaration of a new football season. It goes beyond the fun and magic of Halloween.

It's the inchoate sense of transition. The busy harvest season is all but wound up, and with autumn comes the time to relax, reflect, and rejuvenate the spirit. The bounty of the soil has been gathered, and it's time to look with hope toward the tumultuous, occasionally frigid season to come. Providing the backrop for this soulful downshift is a shower of sweet, crisp, and juicy apples.

Even as summer's long, sultry afternoons give way to the early sunsets and sweater-clad evenings of autumn, something wonderful is happening down in the orchard. The brisk nighttime temperatures have brought with them the special brushes which paint the lustre of ripeness onto the bountiful fall fruit. And each week the farmer shows up at the market with still more apples, spanning a full spectrum of enticing hues and consumptive affinities.

One great thing about apples is that they're almost always tasty as is, eaten out of hand. But some usually are better than others.

For eating, look for the sweeter varieties, such as Red Delicious and Cortland. If you prefer a tart apple, you might go for the giant green Mutsu type, similar to a Granny Smith.

For cooking, some perennial favorites include McIntosh, Rome Beauty, and Spartan.

But these are only very loose, very general guidelines. Here once again the farmer knows best. Because the flavor and texture of the apples varies over the course of the harvest, only the grower knows the state of any given variety from one week to the next. So ask.

For the most part, finding a suitably ripe apple is not a difficult task. It should be firm, assertively colored, and crisp. Stay away from mealy apples and those with soft spots, poor color, or a shriveled appearance. Splotchy brown areas on the surface, known as scald, are the result of gases given off by the apples during storage. Unless the scald is extensive, it is harmless and shouldn't affect the quality of the apples.

The By-Products

Along with the orchard's generous bequeathal come a couple of bonus items which certainly warrant some discussion. Both by-products of the adaptable apple, one is a piece of the farmer's handiwork; the other is yours. Between the apples themselves and the cider and sauces made from them, the wealth of the harvest spreads far and wide.

If you're lucky, you can find cider throughout the market season. Like industrious squirrels, some orchardists stock away hoards of cider each fall, not in hollow trees but in enormous freezers, in anticipation of next summer's parched throats. This frozen nectar is indeed a welcome offering at the early summer market, many weeks before the first fresh apples show up on the farmers' tables.

But the real fresh stuff first appears toward the end of summer. It takes several weeks into the harvest for apples to develop sufficient stores of sugar to render the sweet, nourishing pressing of juice which becomes cider. It's worth the wait.

The farmer tends to take considerable pride in his cider. The end result of both his cultivation and pressing skills, the cider is nothing less than a tangible, delectable statement about his professional success.

Apple cider should taste very sweet and rich. A slightly off or yeasty flavor means that the cider has begun to ferment or "harden." Some ciders have deposits which settle at the bottom of the container, making the final glass rather gritty. This sediment is harmless, but not especially refreshing. Feel free to throw it away.

You can use cider in a variety of ways. Mixed into marinades and stews, it can coax chewy meats into tenderness and bring a subtle, sweet-tart zip to the resultant dishes. To use it as a sweetener in baking, boil it down to about one-fourth its original volume and experiment with using it as you would honey. It also makes a tasty replacement for water when used in glazes and pies.

As for applesauce, no other mode of cooking apples is simpler, tastier, or more loyal to the fruit's virtues. Made by merely cooking the apples and separating pulp from seeds, stems, and skin, applesauce is the essence of the crop.

There are numerous ways to make it. Quickest and easiest is simply chunking the whole apple into a large kettle, adding a splash of water, and cooking the whole mess down to a near mush. Then you just sieve or mill the mixture to remove the skin and core debris.

If you want to do a little more work, the seeds can be cut out of the quartered apples before you cook them. This can help prevent the slightly bitter flavor sometimes imparted by the seeds. It isn't mandatory, but it's good insurance for a tasty result.

If you haven't got a good sieve or a food mill, you'll need to peel and core the apples before you make the sauce, simply mashing the cooked pulp or whirling it in a blender or food processor until it is the consistency you like.

Applesauce allows plenty of latitude for individual taste. You can sweeten it with honey or brown sugar if you like, though it's not often necessary. Spice is nice, if you like it. Cinnamon, cloves, ginger, nutmeg, and allspice are all good, in assorted combinations.

Or you can be a little more creative. Try putting in a few ripe pears, letting their sweetness and superb stores of fiber enrich the sauce. I like to use about twice as many apples as pears, but you should experiment to find your own favorite ratio.

Another variation is the marriage of grated zucchini and applesauce. Add the squash to freshly cooked sauce and continue cooking until the zucchini is tender. Season the mixture to taste and then puree it if you want it smoother.

You might also want to try a candy-spiced sauce, made of chopped apples cooked with little cinnamon "red hots." When the candy melts, the sauce is sweet, chunky, spiced, and a beautiful pink— a real treat.

And of course, the excesses of your saucing zeal can be preserved for another day, when the harvest season seems worlds away and the winter winds all too cruel. To can the sauce, fill hot, sterilized jars to within half an inch of the top, seal them, and submerge in a boiling-water bath for ten minutes. When that frigid February morning comes and you reach for an inviting jar of home-canned sauce, open it up and heat it gently, all the effort will have been worthwhile.

Mom's Apple Crisp

There are members of my family who think the hard sauce is the best part of this dessert. I disagree, though the crisp definitely wouldn't be the same without it.

Serves 6–8

6–8 apples, peeled, cored, and sliced
¼ cup water
¾ cup sugar
½ cup pastry or cake flour
1 teaspoon cinnamon
½ teaspoon salt
2 tablespoons softened butter
Hard Sauce (recipe follows)

Preheat the oven to 375°F.

Place the apple slices in a 1-quart baking dish. Add water.

Combine the sugar, flour, cinnamon, and salt; blend in butter until the mixture is crumbly. Spread evenly over the apples.

Bake for an hour at 375°F. Serve warm, with hard sauce on top.

Hard Sauce

2 cups powdered sugar
¼ cup softened butter
¼ teaspoon vanilla
Half & half, as needed

Mix the sugar, butter, and vanilla as best you can. Dribble in the cream, a little at a time, stirring until the mixture resembles soft ice cream. Place in a serving bowl and chill until hardened.

Apple-Rice Pudding

Wholesome and comforting.

Makes 4–6 servings

1¼ cups water
2 tablespoons butter, divided
Pinch of salt
½ cup short-grain brown rice (uncooked)
1 dried pineapple ring, chopped
1 egg, beaten
2 large Rome beauty apples
2 teaspoons honey
½ teaspoon vanilla
Half & Half

Put the water, 1 tablespoon of the butter, and the salt in a small saucepan. Bring to a boil and gradually stir in the rice. Cover tightly and simmer for 35 minutes or until tender. Cool slightly. Stir in the pineapple, then the egg; replace the cover and set aside.

Preheat the oven to 350°F. Peel, core, and chop the apples. Place in a bowl; drizzle with honey and vanilla and toss gently.

Generously butter a 1-quart casserole. Spread half of the apples in the bottom, then put on half of the rice mixture. Repeat. Dot with the remaining tablespoon of butter and bake in the preheated oven for 45–50 minutes, until golden brown. Serve warm, surrounded by a little moat of half & half.

Apple-Zucchini Muffins

Great for a fall tea party or with brunch.

Makes about 18 muffins

1 cup coarsely shredded unpeeled zucchini
3 eggs, well beaten
1½ cups firmly packed brown sugar
1 tablespoon vanilla
1 cup vegetable oil
1 cup coarsely shredded unpeeled apple
1 cup unbleached white flour
1 cup whole-wheat flour
1⅓ cups rolled oats
1¼ teaspoons baking powder
1 teaspoon baking soda
½ teaspoon salt
1 tablespoon cinnamon
½ teaspoon nutmeg
1 cup chopped walnuts (optional)

Set the zucchini in a colander to drain for 15 minutes. Preheat the oven to 400°F.

Beat the eggs, brown sugar, vanilla, and oil together. Squeeze the excess moisture from the zucchini and stir it into the creamed mixture, along with the apple.

Combine the flours, oats, baking powder, soda, salt, cinnamon, and nutmeg. Blend into the batter. Fold in the nuts.

Fill greased muffin tins ¾ full. Bake for 20–25 minutes at 400°F.

Apple Sorbet

A refreshing dessert for an Indian-summer day.

Makes about 1½ quarts

1½ cups apple cider
½ cup sugar
2 pounds firm apples, pared, cored, and sliced
¼ lemon juice
2 tablespoons applejack
¼ teaspoon cinnamon
Pinch of nutmeg

Heat the cider with the sugar, stirring to dissolve sugar completely. Cool and chill.

Put the apple slices in a heavy-bottomed saucepan with enough water to cover them. Cook gently for 10–15 minutes, until soft. Drain and puree in a blender or food processor. Cool and chill.

In the canister of your ice-cream maker, combine the chilled puree, cider mixture, lemon juice, applejack, and spices. Freeze according to the manufacturer's directions.

Cranapple-Nut Loaf

Great for the holidays, but you can make it before then if you like.

Makes 1 loaf

2 cups unbleached white flour
⅓ cup sugar
1 tablespoon baking powder
½ teaspoon nutmeg
½ teaspoon salt
⅔ cup apple cider
2 eggs, lightly beaten
3 tablespoons unsalted butter, melted and cooled
½ cup chopped pecans
¾ cup fresh cranberries, chopped coarse
½ cup chopped, peeled apple
1 teaspoon finely grated lemon peel

Preheat the oven to 350°F. Grease a 9″ × 5″ loaf pan.

Sift together the flour, sugar, baking powder, nutmeg, and salt. Make a well in the center of the dry ingredients; pour in the cider, eggs, and butter. Stir only until well combined. Gently fold in the nuts, cranberries, apple, and lemon peel.

Turn the batter into the prepared pan and bake for 45–50 minutes, or until a knife inserted into the center of the loaf comes out clean. Cool 10 minutes in the pan, then turn out onto a rack to finish cooling.

Apple Graham Crackers

An utterly wholesome snack.

Makes about 2–3 dozen cookies,
depending on the sizes you cut them into

2⅓ cups apple cider
1⅓ cups whole-wheat pastry flour
½ teaspoon baking powder
¼ teaspoon nutmeg
¼ cup unsalted butter, softened
½ teaspoon vanilla
⅓ cup raisins, chopped
Milk

Put the cider in a medium saucepan and cook over medium heat until reduced to ⅓ cup (the reduction may be jelled and quite thick, depending on the sweetness of your cider). Set aside to cool to room temperature.

Mix the flour, baking powder, and nutmeg together; add the butter and rub the mixture with your fingertips until uniformly crumbly. Sprinkle on the vanilla, cider reduction, and raisins; mix with a fork and gather into a ball. Chill briefly if the dough is too sticky to roll out.

Preheat the oven to 350°F

On a floured board, roll the dough out to a thickness of no more than ¼ inch. Cut with floured cookie cutters or slice into squares. Transfer to a greased cookie sheet and prick each cracker a couple of times with a sharp-tined fork. Brush with milk.

Bake the crackers for 8–10 minutes in a 350°F oven. Be careful not to overbake them. Cool on a rack.

Doris's Apple Shake

Doris Dongvillo and her husband, Adolph, have an orchard in southwestern Michigan. This smooth beverage makes good use of the sweet cider they always have on hand.

Serves 6

1 quart cold apple cider
1 pint vanilla ice cream
1 8¾-ounce can crushed pineapple in juice
½ teaspoon cinnamon

Place everything in a blender jar and mix until smooth. Serve immediately.

Cider Stew

This homey supper dish puts out an aroma that is guaranteed to whet the most reluctant appetite.

Serves 6

3 tablespoons flour
1½ teaspoons salt
¼ teaspoon pepper
¼ teaspoon dried thyme
2 pounds stew beef, cut into 2-inch cubes
3 tablespoons vegetable oil
2 cups apple cider
½ cup water
2 tablespoons cider vinegar
2 medium onions, sliced
3 medium potatoes, peeled and thickly sliced
4 medium carrots, peeled and cut into logs
1 rib celery, sliced
2 medium parsnips, scraped and sliced,
  or 1 turnip, peeled, and coarsely chopped
¼ cup chopped parsley

Mix the flour, salt, pepper, and thyme on a plate. Dredge the meat pieces in the seasoned flour.

Heat the oil in a large kettle or dutch oven. Working in batches, brown the meat thoroughly. Drain off the fat, then return the meat to the pan. Add the cider, water, and vinegar, scraping up any bits which have stuck to the bottom of the pan. Cover, bring to a boil, then simmer about 1¼ hours or until the meat is almost tender.

Add the onions, potatoes, carrots, celery, and parsnips. Cover and simmer another 30 minutes or until the vegetables are tender. Sprinkle in the parsley, stir well, and serve.

Applesauce Oatmeal Cake

Humble and old-fashioned, this cake travels well to picnics and such.

Makes one 9-inch square cake

¼ cup oil
⅓ cup honey
1 egg
¾ cup applesauce
1 cup unbleached white flour
⅔ cup rolled oats
½ teaspoon cinnamon
¼ teaspoon each: allspice, cloves, and salt
½ cup raisins
¼ cup chopped walnuts
1 teaspoon soda
¼ cup hot apple cider

Preheat the oven to 350°F
Blend the oil, honey, egg, and applesauce in a large bowl.

Mix the flour, oats, spices, and salt in a small bowl. Toss a spoonful or two of the mixture with the raisins and nuts.

Mix the soda and apple cider together; add to the applesauce mixture alternately with the flour mixture, beginning and ending with the dry ingredients. Fold in the raisins and nuts.

Turn the batter into a greased and floured 9-inch square pan. Bake in the preheated oven for 50 minutes or until a toothpick tests clean. (If the cake seems to be browning too quickly, cover it loosely with foil.) Cool on a rack.

CHAPTER 8

FOOD TO HIBERNATE BY

Well, another summer has come and gone. Now the farmers appear at the market clad in jackets and sweaters, perhaps warm hats and gloves too. Chilly prewinter winds swirl around bins brimming with fall produce, threatening next week's pickings with taunts of frost, perhaps even a flurry of early snowflakes. It's time to stock up for the cold winter months ahead.

Gone are the fresh, sweet, and tender flavors of the early season. It's likely to be several months before you once again bite into a leaf of young lettuce or a nectar-filled peach. These are the days of sturdier goods, foods that will stand up to weeks or even months of conscientious storage. This is the point where you begin to squirrel away the harvest, stockpiling freshness in preparation for winter's agricultural dry spell.

Most of the cellar-bound goods are tubers and root vegetables, subterranean morsels that can tolerate periods of storage without appreciably altering their basic character. These hardy, adaptable crops include potatoes, both sweet and white; parsnips, celeriac, and onions; and a bit more perishably, carrots and turnips.

Potatoes

White potatoes, whether brown- or red-skinned, reach full maturity about this time, though they've been coming to market since childhood. Those tender little new potatoes of early summer are one of the market's greatest treats.

But the grown-up version is also delicious and terrifically versatile, too. At the market, pick firm, well-shaped potatoes with smooth skin. Keep away from the ones with green sunburn spots, which can be bitter or even mildly toxic. Avoid as well those with large cuts or bruises which you would have to pare away, and leathery, discolored, shriveled or sprouting spuds, which are all too old to be worth eating.

If you plan to cook the potatoes together, buy them in reasonably similar sizes so their timing requirements will be about the same. And choose your variety according to your cooking plans: new potatoes are best for boiling; general-purpose spuds boil well but can be baked; waxy redskins are famous for the salads they make; russets are most outstanding baked in their little brown jackets.

White potatoes store nicely, so you can stock up on them a bit. Keep them, unwashed, in a dark, dry, well-ventilated spot at 45–50 degrees. They'll stay quite happy that way for several months. If it's colder, the potatoes' starches turn to sugar. At higher temperatures, they tend to shrivel, soften, and sprout. If your only available storage spot is at room temperature, plan to use the potatoes within a couple of weeks.

Dan's Pioneer Eggs

I can always count on my husband to make this dish, his specialty, for company.

Serves 6

½ pound of bacon
6 medium russet potatoes
½ medium onion, chopped
½ medium green bell pepper, chopped
Salt, pepper, and garlic powder to taste
5–6 eggs
1 cup shredded sharp cheddar cheese

Cook the bacon in a large cast-iron skillet until crisp. Remove from the pan and drain. Pour all but 2 tablespoons of the bacon fat into a heat-proof container and save it.

Wash and dice the potatoes into ½-inch cubes. Sauté them in the skillet until light golden brown and almost tender. Stir in the onion and green pepper and cook until tender, adding a little reserved bacon fat if needed. Season the mixture to taste, then break in the eggs. Stir until partially cooked, then add the cheese and stir until melted. Serve immediately.

Janssen's Temptation

My friend Cindy developed this version of the sinfully rich Swedish dish.

Serves 6

6 large (fist size) redskin potatoes
1 large onion
1 cup sour cream
1 teaspoon anchovy paste
¼ cup melted butter or margarine
Salt and pepper to taste
Snipped chives

Preheat the oven to 350°F.

Wash and dry the potatoes. Slice them crosswise very thinly, cutting only about ¼ inch from the bottom skin; be careful not to cut all the way through. Place the potatoes, cuts facing up, in a greased 8-inch baking dish. Slice the onion into very thin rings and spread them around on top of the potatoes. Cover the dish and bake at 350°F for 45 minutes, or until the potatoes are fork-tender.

As soon as the potatoes go into the oven, mix the sour cream, anchovy paste, butter, salt, and pepper. Set aside to come to room temperature.

When the potatoes are done, pour the sour cream mixture over them and replace the cover. Return the dish to the oven, turn the oven off, and leave it all alone for 5–7 minutes. Serve at once, sprinkled with chives.

Potato Pancakes

Serves 5–6

2 eggs
1 cup milk
3 large potatoes, peeled and chopped
1 medium onion, chopped
1 medium clove garlic, minced
Salt to taste
1 cup flour
Butter and oil
Garnishes: sour cream, sliced scallions, crumbled bacon

Put the eggs, milk, potatoes, onion, garlic, and salt in a blender jar and blend until creamy smooth.

Transfer the mixture to a medium bowl and add flour gradually, stirring until a workable batter consistency is reached.

Heat a large, heavy skillet and put about a teaspoon each of butter and vegetable oil in it. Mix as the butter melts. Fry pancakes in the mixture until golden brown on both sides. Keep hot in a warm oven while you fry the rest, replenishing the oil-butter mixture as needed.

Top each pancake with a dollop of sour cream and a sprinkling of scallions and bacon. Serve hot.

Grill-Baked Redskins

The waxy character of redskin potatoes is well suited to the barbecue grill. It's convenient to be able to cook all the meal's hot foods on the grill, keeping your kitchen free from the heat.

Serves 6

2 pounds redskin potatoes
½ medium onion, chopped
6 tablespoons cold butter
Salt and pepper to taste
¼ cup chopped parsley
1 teaspoon chopped fresh marjoram or dill (optional)

Wash the potatoes and cut into 1-inch chunks (if they're small, halve them or even leave them whole). Place on a large sheet of heavy-duty foil. Sprinkle on the onion, then distribute slivers of butter over the vegetables. Season with salt and pepper; spread the herbs over everything. Wrap tightly in foil and place on the grill. Cook for 35–45 minutes, turning once, until tender.

Sweet Potatoes

Sweet potatoes, a mainstay of the fall harvest, are root vegetables stuffed full of vitamin A and complex carbohydrates. Their natural sugars complement a wide variety of other flavors, making them a good candidate for casseroles.

In shopping for them, choose well-shaped, bright-colored and firm specimens exhibitng no signs of blemish or decay. Sweet potatoes may show decay with the presence of worm holes, cuts, or injury which penetrates their skin, or with soft and wet or dry and shriveled areas. Occasionally sweet potatoes will have small, dark spots, perhaps running together to form large splotches. These marks are harmless and can be removed with the peel. Oddly shaped potatoes and those with hollow cracks also are nonthreatening, though they do entail a lot of undue waste.

Store your sweet potatoes in a cool area, at around 60 degrees or lower, for up to two months. At room temperature, they'll keep for about a week.

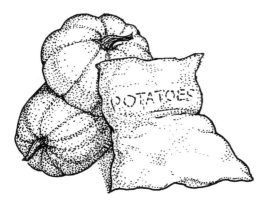

Bourbon Sweet Potatoes

My Aunt Bev has a wonderful Southern drawl to match the flavor of this dish she originated.

Serves 4–6

1½ cups cooked, mashed sweet potatoes
½ cup sugar
¼ cup milk
¼ cup bourbon
1 egg, beaten
¼ teaspoon salt
1 teaspoon vanilla
Topping (recipe follows)

Mix well and put in a buttered casserole. Sprinkle with topping and bake in 350°F oven for 30 minutes. Serve hot.

Topping

½ cup light brown sugar
½ cup chopped pecans
¼ cup flour
¼ cup butter, not softened

Mix sugar, nuts, and flour; cut in butter until crumbly.

Sweet Potato–Carrot Dip

A little bit sweet, a little bit savory, this vitamin A–rich mixture lacks the fat and calories of routine party dips.

Makes about 2 cups

½ pound carrots, peeled and chunked
½ pound sweet potatoes, peeled and chunked
2 medium cloves garlic, unpeeled
1 teaspoon cumin
½ teaspoon cinnamon
2 tablespoons olive oil
1½ tablespoons wine vinegar
Breadsticks

Put the carrots, sweet potatoes, and garlic into lightly salted boiling water and cook until soft, about 15 minutes. Drain. Remove the garlic cloves and slip off the skins. Place the vegetables and the remaining ingredients in a blender or food processor and puree until smooth. Chill until ready to serve. Surround with good crisp breadsticks.

Parsnips

Parsnips are a true fall crop—hardy, humble, and homey. They rank among the harvest's most sorely underrated goods.

Long favored for adding to wintry soups and stews, parsnips also do delicious duty when grated raw into salads, cut into sticks for inclusion with crudités, or even cooked, mashed, and added to savory sauces and gravies as a thickening agent. They're quite tasty cooked simply, sautéed in butter and finished off with little salt and pepper. And for a sweet treat, try cooking and glazing them as you would carrots.

Look for medium-size, smooth, firm parsnips. Very large ones might have flavorless, woody cores. Wilted or flabby parsnips can be fibrous and pithy, perhaps even decayed.

The advancing frosts of autumn seem to inject bonuses of sweet flavor into parsnips, so the later you buy them, the better they're likely to be.

Parsnips will keep well for a couple of months layered in damp sand or stored in a cool root cellar. If you have no such storage facilities, plan to hold them in the refrigerator no longer than a week.

Parsnips Baked with Fruit

A hearty and unusual side dish.

Serves 6

1 pound parsnips
2 large, tart apples
1 large navel orange, peeled
1 teaspoon grated orange rind
3 tablespoons butter, melted
2 tablespoons brown sugar
3 tablespoons orange juice
Dash of nutmeg

Preheat the oven to 350°F.

Peel the parsnips and cut into three-inch lengths, splitting the larger portions to make all of the pieces about equal in size. Core, peel, and thickly slice the apples. Slice the orange crosswise into 10–12 slices. Put the parsnips, fruit, and rind into a large bowl.

Mix the butter, brown sugar, orange juice, and nutmeg. Drizzle over the vegetables and toss gently. Turn the mixture into a buttered casserole. Cover and bake for 30 minutes at 350°F. Uncover and bake 10 minutes longer. Baste with the juices in the dish and serve hot.

Celeriac

Celeriac, or celery root, also falls on the list of underexploited roots, perhaps because its gnarly appearance seems intimidating to the neophyte. That's a shame, because underneath that hideous, knobby surface lies a smooth, celery-like vegetable which is most tasty.

Although there is much waste with this root—thick peelings need to be removed with the aid of a good sharp knife—the tops provide a plus: slender ribs and leaves which can be used to replace celery in enriching stocks and soups. You can even slice them off and freeze them in plastic bags, pulling out a handful or two of the stalks as you need them.

Celery root is a tasty, potent addition to winter stews. Do use it sparingly. It adds great flavor to potato dishes and brings new zip, grated and left raw, folded into a Waldorf salad. It does discolor rapidly, so as you cut it up, pop it into a bowl of cold water to which you have added a little vinegar or fresh lemon juice.

At the market, choose nicely rounded roots no bigger than a softball. Larger roots may be woody and flavorless. Leave behind any celeric which is soft or withered.

Celeriac can be stored for about two months if you layer it in sand and store it in a cool cellar. Like parsnips, it will keep for just a week or so in the refrigerator.

Celeriac Salad

A simple, late-season cousin of cole slaw.

Serves 4–6

1 pound celery root
1½ tablespoons wine vinegar
2½ tablespoons mayonnaise
2 teaspoons Dijon mustard
1 tablespoon heavy cream
1½ teaspoons fresh tarragon, chopped (½ teaspooon dried)
Salt and pepper to taste

Peel the tough outer rind from the celeriac with a sharp paring knife. Cut the flesh into julienne strips, dropping them into a large bowl of cold water as you go.

Drain the celeriac and toss with the vinegar. Combine the mayonnaise, mustard, cream, tarragon, salt, and pepper. Pour over the celeriac and toss well. Chill for at least an hour before serving.

Onions

Like some of the other fall crops, onions by this time have been coming to market for months. Sweet, pungent, and indispensable, onions are one market item seldom missing from the family table.

Unlike the fragile green leeks and scallions of the early harvest, autumn's crop consists of dry onions, big and crisp and great for storage. They'll keep for two or three months at cool room temperature, but give them a dry spot with room to breathe. Too much moisture or warmth will lead to sprouting or decay.

Choose firm, dry, hard onions with plenty of protective peel. Greenness around the neck end (opposite the hairy root) indicates sprouting—not a good development, because it means bitterness. Avoid onions with severe blemishes or green sunburn spots. Wet onions and those with soft spots also should be left behind. Softness around the neck probably means decay or immaturity. On the other hand, very thick, dry, and woody neck ends indicate that the onions are overaged.

When it comes to handling onions, several tricks are available for dealing with their acrid aura. It helps to cut off the root end first. This seems to release some of the fumes. You can try chopping them with a wet blade, dipping your knife in water periodically as you go. Some people think they're less tear-jerking when chilled, and you might agree. Be sure to refrigerate your onions for a short period only. The moisture of the refrigerator can fuel their urge to sprout.

Other tricks for dry-eyed chopping include wearing ski goggles or stuffing a slice of dry bread in your mouth. You might want to try those methods when no one else is around.

It also helps to buy reasonably fresh onions. These root vegetables gain potency with time, so don't try to store them too long.

Onion-Mushroom Soup

This may seem like a lot of garlic, but the long simmering period gives the cloves a mild, almost sweet flavor.

Serves 6–8

1 tablespoon oil
3 tablespoons butter, divided
1½ pounds onions, peeled and chopped
1 bulb garlic, separated into unpeeled cloves
4 cups chicken stock
2 cups water
½ pound mushrooms, sliced thin
Salt and pepper to taste
½ cup grated Gruyère or other Swiss cheese

Heat the oil and 2 tablespoons of the butter in a large saucepan or stock pot. Sauté the onions gently in it until golden brown.

Meanwhile, put the garlic cloves into a heat-proof bowl and cover them with boiling water. Let them stand for 30 seconds; drain. Rinse with cold water; slip off the skins. Add the garlic, stock, and 2 cups water to the onions. Simmer, covered, for 30 minutes.

While the soup simmers, sauté the mushrooms in the remaining tablespoon of butter until they are soft and the liquid has evaporated. Remove from the heat.

Strain the soup, returning the liquid to the kettle. Puree the onions and garlic in a blender or food processor and return them to the pot. Season to taste. Stir in the sautéed mushrooms. Cover and simmer 10 minutes or more. Serve hot, sprinkled with cheese.

Onion Sauce

Delicious over freshly steamed vegetables and with omelettes.

Makes about 3 cups

5 tablespoons butter
4 cups chopped sweet onions
1 teaspoon salt
¼ cup flour
2 cups milk
White pepper to taste

Melt the butter in a medium saucepan. Add the onions and salt and cook over medium–low heat until very tender, about 20 minutes. Stir in the flour and cook, stirring, for about 2–3 minutes. Whisk in the milk and increase the heat. Stirring constantly, bring to a boil. Turn the flame back down and simmer 15 minutes, stirring occasionally.

Puree the sauce in a blender or food processor. Return to the cooking pot, add white pepper to taste, and reheat.

Stuffed Onions

Encasing a meat filling within a big, sweet bulb makes a delicious flavor combination.

Serves 4

4 large sweet onions
3 tablespoons butter
2 cloves garlic, minced
1 rib celery, chopped fine
¼ cup finely chopped green pepper
1 pound ground round
½ teaspoon thyme
Pinch of marjoram
Salt and pepper to taste
½ cup fresh bread crumbs
1 cup beef broth

Preheat oven to 375°F.

Slice the root end of the onions flat so they will sit upright by themselves, taking care not to cut all the way through. Cut off the other end and hollow out the onions with a melon baller or a small spoon, leaving walls about ⅜ inch thick. Save the innards, and be careful not to poke a hole in the bottom.

Drop the onion shells into a kettle of boiling water and leave for 3 minutes. Drain and cool upside down on a rack.

Chop the onion scoopings and sauté them in the butter along with the garlic, celery, and green pepper until barely tender. Remove from the pan with a slotted spoon. Put the beef into the still-hot pan; crumble and brown it. Drain off any excess fat, replace the sautéed vegetables, and add seasonings.

Spoon the beef mixture into the onion shells. Place in a baking dish just large enough to hold them and top with the bread crumbs. Pour the broth into the bottom of the dish. Bake at 375°F for 40–50 minutes. Serve hot.

Garlic

Closely related to the onion, and equally maligned for its good-natured pungency, is garlic. And it's every bit as crucial an item for the hearty dishes which winter inspires.

Like onions, garlic comports itself when cooked very differently from its raw state. Each form has its place.

Pleasantly piquant, raw garlic enlivens salads, dressings, and sauces with its inimitable spunk. But cook it for a bit, and the bodacious bulb becomes mild, sweet, and aromatic—altogether tame. It ceases to carry the dreaded breath-tainting trait of raw garlic. This Jekyll-Hyde aspect is often ignored by those who insist that garlic must be avoided by anyone planning to socialize with other human beings.

When properly matured, garlic is dry and firm, its outer surface covered with crackly skin. You should avoid soft, spongy, or dirty garlic.

It also makes sense to buy bulbs with large cloves. Peeling the skin off of tiny garlic cloves can be sheer headache-inspiring tedium.

If you cut open a garlic clove and find a green shoot growing within, pull it out and discard it. The rest of the clove is probably fine, but the sprout would make it bitter.

The more you use garlic, the more user-friendly it seems to become. Handling the cloves isn't difficult, once you're accustomed to it. It's certainly not enough of a nuisance to justify substituting powdered or granulated garlic for the real thing with any regularity. Their flavor cannot compare with the fresh version, and they should be strictly forbidden in dishes where the garlic plays any significant part.

Peeling garlic is quick and easy. Just lay a wide knife blade flat, parallel to your chopping surface, on top of a garlic clove. One quick, gentle-yet-firm tap on the side of the blade with the side of your fist, and the skin will slide right off.

Many cookbooks recommend pressing garlic, but I find that squashing the cloves in a torture apparatus produces a faintly bitter taste that I don't detect in chopped garlic. But I'll leave that up to you.

Blender Aioli

This pungent Middle Eastern sauce celebrates garlic. Traditionally served atop lightly steamed or raw vegetables, it also goes well with grilled or baked fish. A garnish of chopped chives is pretty.

Makes about 2 cups

¼ cup fresh lemon juice
¼ teaspoon salt
½ teaspoon soy sauce
2–3 medium cloves garlic, chopped coarse
1 egg
1 egg yolk
¾ cup olive oil
½ cup vegetable or corn oil

Put the lemon juice, salt, soy sauce, garlic, egg, and yolk in a blender jar. Whirl on high speed until smooth. Combine the oils and, with the blender running on medium speed, dribble them very gradually into the egg-garlic mixture, stopping as soon as all the oil is added. The sauce should be creamy and thick. Serve immediately.

Carrots

Carrots are another of the crops which appear through the market season. From the pinky-sized cylinders of late spring to the sturdy orange batons of autumn, they form a staple of the farmer's fare.

An attractive addition to soups, stews, stir-fries, and salads, carrots bring with them generous amounts of vitamin A, potassium, and carbohydrates. Unlike most vegetables, carrots are more nutritious cooked than raw. Cooking softens their relatively tough cellular walls, releasing their carotene, which the body then converts into vitamin A. Although raw carrots are certainly a wholesome snack, the human digestive system cannot break down their nutritional components quickly enough, so most of their vitamins and minerals end up passing through the body without being absorbed. When you shop for carrots, look for a smooth surface and a deep orange color. The deeper the color, the more vitamin A there is inside. The top greenery should be fairly fresh-looking, but if there are lots of stems coming out of the tops, the carrots probably have large, tough cores and should be left with the farmer. Very large carrots also are likely to have big cores. Other undesirable signs are wilting, shriveling, and surface cracks. Carrots with prominently forked roots or numerous little roots are probably more mature than you want them to be.

It is possible to store carrots for the winter hibernation period, but you need a humid root cellar with 35- to 45-degree temperatures. If you have such a spot, store your carrots there, trimmed and layered in boxes of moist sand, for up to about three months. If your cellar is too warm, keep your carrots, loosely covered, their tops and tips removed, in the refrigerator for up to two weeks.

There are lots of ways to prepare carrots for cooking, possibly more than there are for any other vegetable. You can chop or shred them for salads or casseroles. Cut into uniformly sized logs, they cook evenly and look inviting stacked on a plate or sprinkled throughout a stew.

For stir-frying, peel the carrots and then slice them, knife held at a diagonal angle, rolling the carrots about 90 degrees between cuts. This "roll cut" technique exposes more of their surface area to the heat, allowing them to cook more quickly and absorb more of the flavors of the other foods cooked with them.

To serve carrots plain, I like to slice them diagonally, about ¼ inch thick, and then steam them. Add a little melted butter and some chopped parsley or tarragon and you have an easy, gorgeous side dish.

Carrot Bread

This is a teatime version of carrot cake. If you miss the frosting, spread slices of this dense, sweet bread with softened cream cheese.

Makes one 9" × 5" loaf

1 cup sugar
⅔ cup vegetable oil
2 eggs
1½ cups flour
1 teaspoon baking soda
1 teaspoon baking powder
¼ teaspoon salt
1 teaspoon cinnamon
1 cup grated carrots
1 cup chopped walnuts or pecans

Preheat the oven to 375°F.

Combine the sugar, oil, and eggs; blend thoroughly.

Sift the dry ingredients together and add to the creamed mixture. Stir in the carrots and nuts.

Spread the batter evenly in a greased and floured loaf pan. Bake at 375°F for 55 minutes. Cool in the pan on a wire rack.

Beef Daube

The carrots are a strong costar in this wintry French stew.

Serves 6

¾ cup flour
2 pounds stew beef, cut into 2-inch cubes
3 large carrots, peeled and sliced
2 large onions, halved and sliced
1 28-ounce can tomatoes, drained (save the liquid) and mushed
  by hand
¼ cup gin or vodka
1½ cups beef stock (preferably homemade)
2 tablespoons olive oil
2 medium cloves garlic, chopped fine
1 large bay leaf
½ teaspoooon thyme
2 teaspoon salt
Pepper to taste
½ pound thin-sliced bacon

Preheat the oven to 350°F.

Put the flour on a plate and dredge the meat in it, shaking off excess flour. Set aside.

In a large bowl, mix the carrots, onions, tomatoes, gin (or vodka), stock, oil, garlic, bay leaf, thyme, salt, and pepper.

Take a large, heavy casserole with a cover and line it with the bacon slices, using a little more than half of them. Using a slotted spoon, spread on ⅓ of the vegetable mixture, then ⅓ of the floured beef cubes. Make two more layers; arrange the bacon slices over the top. Pour the vegetable liquid over all, adding some of the reserved tomato juice if needed to cover the stew. Bake for an hour at 350°F, then reduce the heat to 300°F and bake 2 hours longer. Serve over rice or noodles.

Carrot Nut Muffins

These muffins can be frozen for up to a month. Thaw them, covered, at room temperature. If you like, you can reheat them, wrapped in aluminum foil, for about 15 minutes at 350°F.

Makes 12 muffins

1½ cups all-purpose flour
½ cup whole-wheat flour
¼ cup firmly packed brown sugar
1 teaspoon baking powder
½ teaspoon baking soda
¾ teaspoon cinnamon
¾ teaspoon nutmeg
½ teaspoon salt
¾ cup grated carrots
⅓ cup chopped walnuts or pecans
1 cup buttermilk
1 egg
2 tablespoons melted butter

Preheat the oven to 350°F.

Combine the flours, brown sugar, baking powder, soda, spices, and salt in a large bowl, mixing with your fingertips to break up the brown sugar. Blend in the carrots and nuts.

Combine the buttermilk, egg, and butter; stir into the dry ingredients just until everything is moistened.

Fill paper cup–lined muffin tins ⅔ full. Bake the muffins for 30 minutes, or until a toothpick inserted in the center comes out clean.

Turnips and Rutabagas

Turnips and their earthbound cousins, rutabagas, are fall market favorites. Excellent additions to casseroles and stews, they also are delicious braised, baked, mashed, or nestled in alongside roast meats. And they also can be used to enrich stir-fried dishes and salads, or even in mixtures to be used as meat stuffings. Be inventive.

These roots also hold their own when served solo. Simply diced and sautéed, they make a side dish capable of dispelling all notions that turnips and rutabagas should inspire a reflexive crinkling of the nose.

Like carrots, turnips should come topped with a crown of spring greens. And like celeriac, those greens should be saved for another use. (See Chapter 1.)

Buy turnips and rutabagas which are moderately sized, firm of flesh, and rather heavy. Very large, wrinkly, or excessively blemished roots should be avoided.

In turnips, look for no more than a few leaf scars around the purple crown end. The best turnips are small ones, about two inches across, and these appear at the farmers market from mid-summer onward. The older, larger ones found in the fall keep longer, but that is because they are not as tender and moist. They also may have a bitter flavor you're not likely to encounter in a more youthful turnip.

Rutabagas and older turnips store reasonably well in a dry, cool environment, perhaps 60 degrees or cooler. Do check them frequently for softening, though they may be quite content stored this way for three months or more. Very young turnips should be kept in the refrigerator for no more than a week or so.

Sautéed Turnips Elizabeth

This simple approach can make a turnip fan of almost anybody.

Serves 4

1 pound turnips, peeled and cut into ½-inch cubes
6 tablespoons butter
1 large shallot, minced
2 tablespoons chopped parsley
Salt and pepper to taste

Boil the turnips in lightly salted water until just tender, about 8 minutes. Drain.

Melt the butter in a skillet and sauté the shallot in it until tender. Add the turnips and stir to coat; heat through. Stir in the parsley, season to taste, and serve hot.

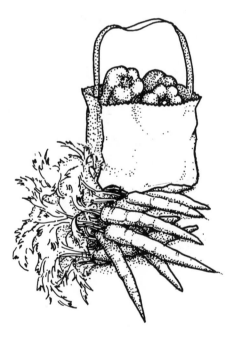

Harvest Pie

Another invention of my chef friend Beth, this crustless pie is a tribute to the bounty of autumn.

Serves 6–8

Softened butter
1½ cups fine, dry bread crumbs
1 cup finely grated cheddar cheese, divided
½ pound turnips, peeled and sliced very thin
2 large carrots, peeled and sliced very thin
2 medium potatoes, peeled and sliced very thin
1 cup half & half
1 egg
¼ cup chopped parsley
Salt and pepper to taste
2 tablespoons chilled butter

Preheat the oven to 400°F. Heavily grease a pie pan with the softened butter.

Mix the bread crumbs with ½ cup of the cheese and sprinkle half or a little more of the mixture over the bottom and sides of the buttered pie plate. Layer half of the turnips, half of the carrots, half of the potatoes, and half of the remaining cheese in the pan. Repeat.

Beat the half & half, egg, and parsley together; pour over the vegetables slowly, allowing it to seep through and poking things around carefully with a fork as necessary to let the mixture through. Sprinkle with the remaining crumb-cheese mixture and dot with slivers of chilled butter.

Bake for 45 minutes, tenting the pie with foil if it begins to brown too quickly. Serve hot.

Rutabaga Custard Pie

A smooth, mellow departure from pumpkin pie.

Serves 6–8

¾ pound rutabaga
2 large, ripe pears
1 tablespoon pure maple syrup
½ teaspoon coriander
¼ teaspoon ginger
⅛ teaspoon nutmeg
Pinch of salt
2 eggs, beaten
2 tablespoons dark brown sugar
1 cup half & half
1 9-inch pie crust, partially baked
Whipped cream

Preheat the oven to 400°F.

Wash and peel the rutabaga, using a sharp paring knife. Cut it into 1-inch chunks. Place in a pan over hot water and steam for about 20 minutes. Peel, quarter, and core the pears; add to the rutabagas and steam 10 minutes longer or until very tender. Puree the mixture in a blender, food processor, or food mill, then blend in the syrup, spices, and salt. Mix well.

In a large bowl, beat the eggs and brown sugar together until thick and lemon-colored. Mix in the rutabaga mixture. Add the half & half and blend thoroughly. Turn into the prebaked crust. Bake at 400°F for 15 minutes, then reduce the heat to 350°F and bake 25–30 minutes longer, until the custard is set. Cool the pie on a wire rack. Serve topped with whipped cream.

Rutabaga, Country Style

Homey and tummy-warming, this dish can be part of a major feast or serve as the vegetable in a simple fall supper.

Serves 4

1½ pounds rutabaga
¼ pound thick-sliced bacon
½ medium onion, chopped
Pepper to taste

Peel the rutabaga with a small, sharp knife. Cut it into chunks and steam or boil until very tender, about 20–25 minutes. Drain well, then return to the pan and set over low heat for a minute or two to evaporate any excess moisture. Mash with a potato masher until the mixture is only a little bit lumpy.

While the rutabaga is cooking, dice up the bacon into ¼-inch pieces and fry it in a large skillet until crisp. Remove from the pan with a slotted spoon; drain on paper towels.

Pour off all but 3 tablespoons of the bacon fat. Sauté the onion in it gently until tender. Add the mashed rutabaga, the bacon, and pepper to taste. Mix well and heat through. Serve hot.

EPILOGUE

Home Again, Home Again, Farm-Fresh Potato

The fields stand bare. The summer's growth has been gathered and its detritus churned under to bolster the soil for the spring planting. Numerous blizzards and countless frigid gusts stand between now and the day when seeds once again will meet just-thawed earth. Then it all will begin anew.

For now, the cellar is stocked, the shelves laden with jars of preserved goods. Jams and jellies wait patiently for winter's warm bakery to receive their sweet treatment. Pickles line up in tall glass columns, ready to finish off mile-high sandwich platters for eating in front of televised bowl games and hockey playoffs.

Indoors, projects which have piled up over the market season sit waiting for the farmer's attention. It's time to shift into winter gear.

Next year, there may be some changes. Half an acre more asparagus, a couple hundred fewer squash plants. Maybe we'll move up the first spraying in the orchard by a week or so. Or perhaps we'll try a couple new varieties of tomato. The customers seemed to clamor for more tomatoes this year.

Mostly, we've got to keep working toward driving home an empty truck from the market each week.

But for now, it's time to take it easy. Next year can be dealt with later on. Changes or no changes, the people will be back. They always come back.

After all, you've got to eat.

INDEXES

Given here are two more resources for use in your farmers-market consumerism, two guides to the contents of this book.

One is simply an alphabetical list of recipe titles. The other, a bit more comprehensive, is a cross-referenced list of ingredients, whether playing lead or supporting roles. In some cases, even the extras are listed. Generally, recipe titles are given outright where the crop in question is a starring factor (even if its name doesn't appear on the marquee).

Then, in many instances, a section headed "*in:*" will follow, giving additional dishes where that ingredient is used in a less prominent role. The intent here is to enable you to look up a crop which is sitting in your refrigerator and come away with several ideas for using it, deliciously.

Of course, space doesn't allow us to list every ingredient's every appearance. An item of the harvest is listed with recipes just when it is included in the dish in some significant quantity. Onions, for example, appear in many, many of these recipes. But the dishes listed in the index below "Onions" are limited to those preparations which notably highlight the root's inimitable character.

So take these listings as a gentle source of direction. Look several places before you give up. And bring along your imagination. It's one of your most precious natural resources.

Index to Recipe Titles

Index

Purees, as baby food, 149

Quiche, Spinach, 22–23

Radiccio, 18
Radishes, 27
  Spring Radish Spread, 30
  in: Stuffed Brussels Sprouts, 54
Raspberries, 68–70
  Fresh Raspberry Pudding, 81
  Fresh Raspberry Soup, 79
  Raspberry Bread, 80
  Raspberry-Rhubarb Muffins, 78
Redskin potatoes, 170, 172, 174
  Grill-Baked Redskins, 174
    in: Cream of Sorrel Soup, 38; Cream of
    Spinach and Basil Soup, 24
Rhubarb, 13–17
  baked, 13
  Grandma's Rhubarb Coffee Cake, 14
  Raspberry-Rhubarb Muffins, 78
  Rhubarb-Banana Bread Pudding, 15
  Rhubarb Cheesecake, 16
  Rhubarbecue Sauce, 17
Rice, pesto with, 37
Rice Pudding, Apple-, 159
Romaine lettuce, 18
  Easier Caesar Salad, 25
Root vegetables, 169–97
  See also individual listings
Rosemary, 36
    in: Eggplant Roulade, 100–101;
    Eggplant Salsa, 102
Roulade, Eggplant, 100–101
Rutabaga, 193, 196–97
  Rutabaga, Country Style, 197
  Rutabaga Custard Pie, 196

Sage, 36
  in Routissons, 44
Salad dressings
  Celery Seed, 134
  Creamy Caesar, 25
  Cucumber-Dill, 98
  Orange Vinaigrette, 28
  Vinaigrette, 105
  Walnut Vinaigrette, 55
Salad greens, 18

Salads
  Asparagus Vinaigrette with Leeks, 9
  Baby Potato Salad, 127
  Broccoli-Corn Salad, 49
  Broccoli Salad, 49
  Brussels Sprout Leaves with Walnut
    Vinaigrette, 55
  Celeriac Salad, 181
  Cucumber-Yogurt Salad, 98
  Easier Caesar Salad, 25
  French Green Bean Salad, 88
  Fruit-Pasta Salad, 134
  Leeks and Peas with Orange Vinaigrette, 28
  Marinated Tomato Salad, 125
  Overnight Fruit Compote, 63
  Purple Cauliflower Salad, 128
  Quick Slaw McGraw, 52
  Rice Salad Florentine, 22
  Summer Squash Salad, 115
  Tabouli, 122
  Tortellini-Pesto Primavera, 133
Sauces
  Blender Aioli, 187
  Blender Bernaise, 43
  Fresh Tomato-Mozzarella Sauce, 131
  Hard Sauce, 158
  Onion Sauce, 184
  Pesto, 42
  Rhubarbecue Sauce, 17
  Salsa Fresca, 113
  Sauce Aurore, 100–101
Savory, 36
Savoy cabbage, 47
Scallions, 27
    in: Fettucine with Chicken and Aspar-
    agus, 132; Fresh Herb Biscuits, 39;
    Fresh Pea Soup, 104; Potato Pancakes,
    173; Salsa Fresca, 113; Stuffed Squash
    Blossoms Tempura, 129; Summer
    Squash Salad, 115; Tabouli, 122
Shallots
    in: Blender Bernaise Sauce, 43; Cream
    of Sorrel Soup, 38; Eggplant Roulade,
    100–101; Sautéed Turnips Elizabeth, 194
Shrimp
  Ragout of Shrimp with Three Peppers, 112
  Shrimp and Snow Peas, 107
Sorbet, Apple, 161